South

Londo

Patrick Hamilton

30 enjoyable walks for the whole family

Capital Travel Books

First published in 2010 by
Capital Travel Books
PO Box 60167
London SW19 3RX

© Capital Travel Books 2010

All rights reserved. No part of this publication may be reproduced, stored in a retrieval system or transmitted in any form or by any means, electronic, mechanical, photocopying, recording or otherwise without the prior permission of the publisher.

Every effort has been made to ensure that the information in this guide is accurate; however, the publisher cannot be held responsible for any errors, or any problems encountered by readers. The walks in this book were devised and written in 2009 and 2010, and have all been updated before publication, but details of any inaccuracies, or any comments about the walks, would be welcome.

ISBN 978-0-9559537-1-2

Printed by Intype Libra, London SW19 4HE

Maps reproduced by permission of Ordnance Survey on behalf of HMSO. © Crown copyright 2010. All rights reserved. Ordnance Survey Licence number 100048320

Front Cover: Cattle pound at the Green Man, Putney Heath (Walk 30).
Back Cover: The Grenadier, Wilton Row; Young's Brewery, Wandsworth; Beverley Brook; Chelsea Harbour.

Contents

Introduction 4
Location of the walks 5
Walk Record Chart 6

The walks:
1 St James's Park and Green Park. 2 miles. 9
2 Pimlico and Westminster. 4¼ miles. 13
3 Belgravia. 2¾ miles. 21
4 The Serpentine and Kensington Gardens. 3¼ miles. 27
5 Brompton and Knightsbridge. 3 miles. 33
6 Chelsea. 3½ miles. 39
7 Earl's Court. 2¾ miles. 45
8 Walham Green and World's End. 3½ miles. 49
9 Fulham. 4 miles. 55
10 Putney Bridge and Wandsworth. 2½ miles. 61
11 Roehampton and Putney. 3½ miles. 65
12 Mortlake and East Sheen. 4½ miles. 69
13 Barnes and Beverley Brook. 4 miles. 75
14 Wandsworth Common. 4¼ miles. 81
15 Battersea. 5½ miles. 85
16 Stockwell. 3 miles. 91
17 Clapham Park and Brixton. 2½ miles. 95
18 Clapham. 4 miles. 99
19 Balham and Tooting Bec. 4¾ miles. 105
20 King George's Park. 2½ miles. 109
21 Earlsfield and Tooting. 4¼ miles. 113
22 Streatham. 3 miles. 119
23 Norbury. 3¼ miles. 125
24 Colliers Wood and Morden Hall Park. 2½ miles. 129
25 Merton Park. 2¼ miles. 133
26 West Wimbledon. 2¾ miles. 139
27 Wimbledon. 3 miles. 143
28 Wimbledon Common. 4½ miles. 149
29 Cannizaro Park. 2 miles. 153
30 Putney Heath. 4¼ miles. 157

Introduction

If you want to keep fit, go for a walk, so we are often told. And if that walk can be a pleasure rather than a chore, so much the better. The emphasis in this book of London walks is on pointing out interesting buildings, streets, and localities (with a little local history included), and exploring the many public parks and commons that south-west London is blessed with. For those with young children, or limited mobility, details of steps, gradients, and the surface underfoot are mentioned, as are toilets, cafés, and pubs *en route*. Public transport options are listed, along with the approximate distance and time required for each walk, all of which are within fare zones 1-4. A select few of the routes are adapted from walks previously published in *Walking Across London*, Capital Travel Books 2008.

All the walks can be enjoyed on any day of the week but remember that some facilities are restricted on Sundays, including public transport. Virtually all of the walks include a playground to keep the children happy, and somewhere, often in delightful surroundings, to picnic. Finally, there are just a few practical considerations: wear your most comfortable shoes (this is vital; pavements and tarmac can be tiring on the feet), do some planning beforehand so that hunger and thirst are kept at bay, and always take a street atlas, which will prove handy to confirm your route along the way, and essential if a road or path is closed, which can happen for any number of reasons. Be prepared for names, particularly of pubs and cafés, to have changed. The sketch maps included with each walk are intended only as a general guide, and denote some places mentioned in the text with a Δ symbol.

Leafing through the book's pages will hopefully have whetted your appetite to try the walks, so once you're all set, pop the book in a pocket or rucksack, jump on the Tube, train, or bus, and let *South-West London Walks* be your guide.

Location of the walks

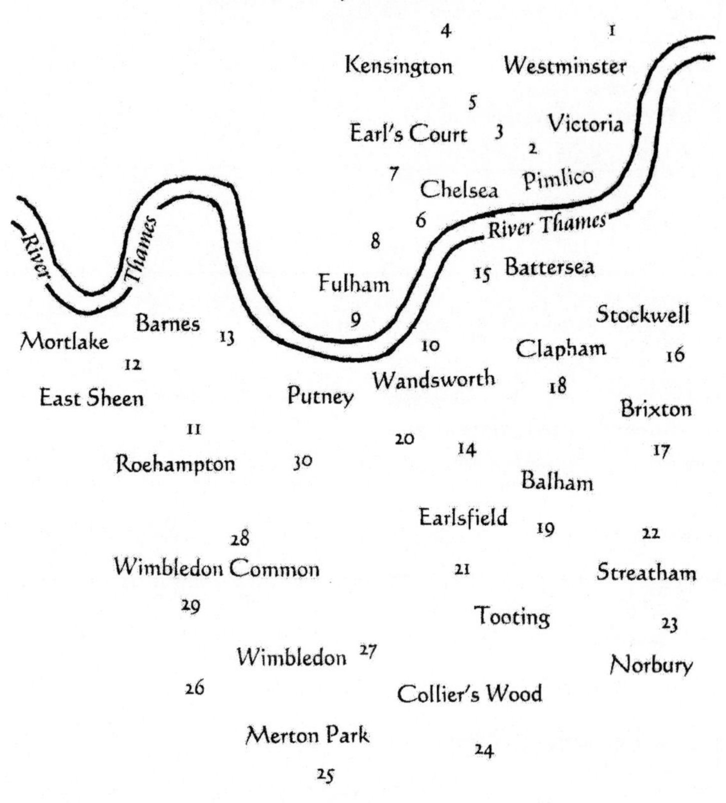

Walk Record Chart

Make a note of when you completed each walk, whether the sun shone, and any other comments here

1 St James's Park and Green Park
2 Pimlico and Westminster
3 Belgravia
4 The Serpentine and Kensington Gardens
5 Brompton and Knightsbridge
6 Chelsea
7 Earl's Court
8 Walham Green and World's End
9 Fulham
10 Putney Bridge and Wandsworth

Walk Record Chart

11 Roehampton and Putney
12 Mortlake and East Sheen
13 Barnes and Beverley Brook
14 Wandsworth Common
15 Battersea
16 Stockwell
17 Clapham Park and Brixton
18 Clapham
19 Balham and Tooting Bec
20 King George's Park

Walk Record Chart

21 Earlsfield and Tooting
22 Streatham
23 Norbury
24 Colliers Wood and Morden Hall Park
25 Merton Park
26 West Wimbledon
27 Wimbledon
28 Wimbledon Common
29 Cannizaro Park
30 Putney Heath

SWI

1 St James's Park and Green Park

A glorious foray into some of the most delightful parkland scenery that the capital has to offer, and a chance to soak up the grandeur of Buckingham Palace

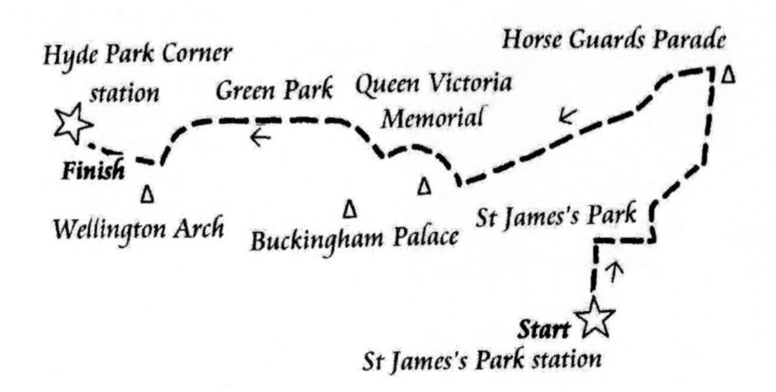

Distance	2 miles.
Time	1-1½ hours.
Terrain	Tarmac and paved paths with one short slope; one flight of steps, easily avoided.
Food and drink	Two or three cafés and pubs near St James's Park station, with several kiosks, and one café, on the way.
Toilets	St James's Park and Hyde Park Corner.
Start	St James's Park station. District and Circle lines. In close proximity to the station, Buses 11, 24, 148, 211 stop near the junction of Victoria Street and Broadway, at New Scotland Yard.
Finish	Hyde Park Corner station. Piccadilly line, Buses 9, 10, 14, 19, 22, 52, 74, 137, 414.

From St James's Park station take the exit for Broadway, then use the zebra crossing at Petty France to go ahead along Queen Anne's Gate. Follow this street as it bears round to the right.

A profusion of blue plaques remind the passer-by of the great names that have resided here, in the company of a statue of Queen Anne, which adorns a wall adjacent to number 15. She looks quite sober here, but apparently liked a little tipple, earning her the soubriquet of 'Brandy Nan'. The first part of the street contains terraces dating from around 1704, with exceptional carved decoration on the door hoods, and grotesque faces peering at you from the brickwork.

Queen Anne surveys the scene in Queen Anne's Gate

At the junction with Dartmouth Street, with the Two Chairmen pub opposite, turn left and after 30 yards descend Cockpit Steps on the left. To avoid this, retrace your walk to turn right through Queen Anne's Gate, then right to arrive at the foot of the steps.

Cockpit Steps recalls the days of cock-fighting, when in the 18th century a cock-pit existed here, one of half-a-dozen in London. These are now alive in street names only; Cockpit Yard and Cockspur Street, where spurs could be bought for fighting cocks; and Cock Hill, where the birds were bred. This age-old entertainment became illegal in 1849.

You emerge from the steps onto Birdcage Walk. Cross directly to a path heading diagonally right across a corner of St James's Park. Keep ahead at a crossing path, then bear left, parallel to Horse Guards Road.

To your right, beside Clive Steps, is the Churchill Museum and Cabinet War Rooms, telling the story of the legendary Sir Winston Churchill and the day-to-day decision making of the Second World War.

Carry on along this path, with a rustic lakeside cottage and Duck Island on your left. Soon you arrive at the Guards Division war memorial, with the open space of Horse Guards Parade to your right. There are toilets a few yards ahead.

To either side of the parade ground are the grand premises of Government; Cabinet Office, Foreign Office, Defence, Treasury, and Parliamentary offices, and a view of the rear of Downing Street's well-protected residences, while located near to the central archway is the Household Cavalry Museum.

At the war memorial turn left into St James's Park and keep going to the 'Inn the Park' café. Fork left here to follow the water's edge.

King James I kept a menagerie of animals here that included crocodiles, camels, and an elephant, and also a collection of exotic birds along Birdcage Walk, and then Charles II added avenues of trees and a long, straight canal. In 1664 the pelicans that are still a feature of the waterside today were given by the Russian Ambassador.

The pelicans of St James's Park

Other unexpected birdlife here includes tawny owls, which breed here, and great spotted woodpeckers, whose staccato drumming you may hear in the treetops. During the 1820s the park was redesigned in a more natural way, without the rigid straight lines, by famous architect John Nash.

At a bridge over the lake (there are toilets to the right here, and a chance to make a detour to see St James's Palace) keep ahead by the waterside. When finally the path swings left before a high wall, turn right up a slope to The Mall.

This vantage point gives you a fine view of Buckingham Palace and the Queen Victoria Memorial. Work on the memorial took 18 years, being finally completed in 1924. Figures representing Truth, Justice, and Motherhood are accompanied by gilded figures of Courage and Constancy, with Victory topping the pillar. The Palace started life as Buckingham House, a red-brick mansion built by John Sheffield, Duke of Buckingham after Arlington House, which previously stood here, was demolished in 1703. The house achieved the title of Palace after rebuilding by John Nash in 1825-36. In 1913 the familiar Portland stone façade was added by Sir Aston Webb, who also designed the memorial. Adjacent to the palace, the Queen's Gallery and the Royal Mews are both open to the public.

Cross The Mall at the pedestrian lights and then follow the back of the stone balustrade as it curves round to the finely crafted, gilded Canada Gates. At the gates turn right into Green Park on the Broad Walk, then after 90 yards, at the second junction, fork left. Stay on this broad path as it undulates its way through the length of the park, passing a tall, lone lamppost.

The Green Park, known as such because of its grassy aspect, is very pleasant, but unassuming. However, the park has a secret past, having been a royal deer-hunting ground in the 17th century, a place where duels were fought, and the venue for tremendous firework displays during national celebrations in the 18th and 19th centuries. It became a public park in 1826.

As your path curves sharply to the left, turn right to leave the park at Hyde Park Corner. Turn left, then right to cross at the lights, heading for the Wellington Arch. Go through the arch, pausing to admire the massive iron gates and fluted Corinthian columns.

Topped with a dramatic bronze statue of Peace, winged and dominant, descending on the chariot of war, Wellington Arch is normally open Wednesday-Sunday, and contains among other exhibits London's smallest police station. Apsley House (the building faced in golden-brown Bath stone to your right) former home of the 'Iron Duke', contains the Wellington Museum, which gives a fascinating insight into the life of the man who achieved victory over Napoleon in 1815 at the Battle of Waterloo.

Walk forward to the Royal Artillery Memorial, one of several sombre memorials grouped on this island site to those who fought and died for our freedom today. Turn right to cross at the lights towards the archway giving access to Hyde Park. The walk ends here, at this convenient spot offering Piccadilly line trains, buses to all parts, toilets a few yards to the left, and most importantly, a tea, coffee, and hot food stall.

The Queen Victoria Memorial

SW1

2 Pimlico and Westminster

For those interested in the buildings of London, both grand and domestic, this long walk will provide a feast of variety and styles down the ages

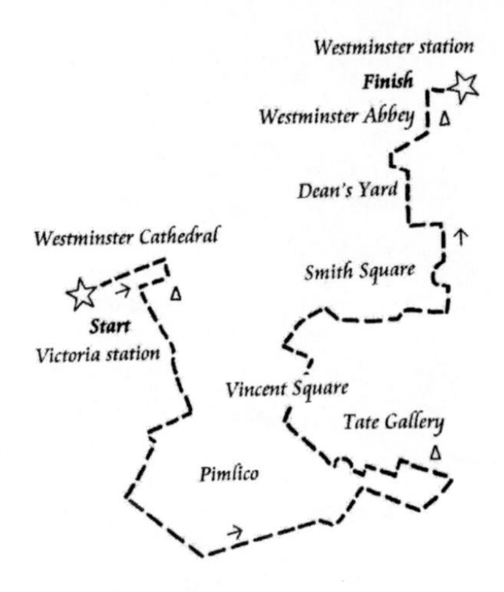

Distance	4¼ miles.
Time	2½-3 hours.
Terrain	Level paving all the way.
Food and drink	Places of refreshment abound in the first mile of the walk, and in Horseferry Road, which is about three-quarters of the way. Near the end, the Methodist Central Hall offers a spacious and sensibly-priced basement café.
Toilets	Victoria station main concourse and near to platform 1, Pimlico, Regency Place, Westminster.
Start	Victoria station. District, Circle, and Victoria lines, frequent trains and buses to all parts.
Finish	Westminster station. District, Circle, and Jubilee lines, Buses 3, 11, 12, 24, 53, 87, 88, 159, 453.

From Terminus Place, Victoria station, turn right to cross Wilton Road and head for 'Little Ben', an ornate clock standing on a traffic island.

Little Ben

French company Elf Aquitaine Ltd. sponsored the reinstatement of Little Ben, which now keeps to British Summer Time, in the spirit of Franco-British friendship. There is an 'Apology for Summer Time' upon the base of the clock; 'My hands you may retard or may advance, my heart beats true for England as for France'. This charming cast-iron timepiece, made by Gillett and Johnston of Croydon in 1892, was removed in 1964 and re-erected in 1981.

Cross Vauxhall Bridge Road and go ahead along Victoria Street, under a covered walkway, to shortly turn right opposite the boldly modern outlines of Cardinal Place to discover the breathtaking sight of Westminster Cathedral.

Distinctively fronted with a sharply-pointed 'nose', Cardinal Place dates from 2005. It possesses in the region of 47,000 square metres of offices, plus shops, cafés, and a roof garden with a restaurant and art gallery. Standing opposite but aloof from the modernity of Victoria Street, Westminster Cathedral, the foremost Roman Catholic church in England, was erected in 1895-1903 to designs by renowned church architect JF Bentley, who did not survive to witness completion of his magnificent project; he died in 1902. Built in an early Christian Byzantine style, the cathedral has a tower 284ft high, and a vast but beautiful interior, rich in fine works of art, marble, and mosaics, and of particular note, a moving set of carvings of the Stations of the Cross by Eric Gill, from 1903-18.

Facing the cathedral, turn sharp right along Ashley Place, then left at Carlisle Place, passing St Vincent's Centre and the monumental but stylish Carlisle Mansions, Cardinal Mansions, and Manning House, which all date from the building boom of the late 1800s. At Francis Street turn right (note a plaque to Cardinal Manning, 1808-1892), cross Vauxhall Bridge Road at the pedestrian lights and turn left, then branch to the right along Upper Tachbrook Street to the shopping thoroughfare of Warwick Way, where you cross over and turn right (to discover a little playground, and public toilets, keep on along Tachbrook Street through the market stalls for 40 yards).

Warwick Way, alive with places to eat, drink, and shop, acts as your introduction to Pimlico, a residential area that stretches to Grosvenor Road and the Thames. Two centuries ago market gardens, producing an abundance of salads, herbs, and vegetables on the well-manured fields of a locality known as the 'Neat Houses' occupied these acres until Thomas Cubitt, who had already successfully developed estates of houses elsewhere in London, negotiated leases with the local landowners and embarked on an ambitious programme of house-building here. That all began in 1824, and construction of the distinguished Italianate 'stucco' (painted plaster) terraces continued apace, even after Cubitt's death in 1855. Nowadays Pimlico, with its wide thoroughfares, relaxed air, and well-kept houses, still retains its original appeal.

Thomas Cubitt

Carry on along Warwick Way, crossing Denbigh Street, then at the junction with Belgrave Road cross over, turn left, then immediately right into Warwick Square, where the gardens (for residents only) form a pleasantly wooded accompaniment to your walk. At St George's Drive turn left, with St Gabriel's church opposite.

Consecrated in 1853, St Gabriel's was designed by Thomas Cundy, surveyor to the Grosvenor Estate, the major local landowner.

Press on, crossing several side roads, to a junction with Denbigh Street, where a statue of master builder Thomas Cubitt (1788-1855), looking ready to get on with some new project, occupies the corner triangle.

Having started in the building trade as a carpenter, Thomas Cubitt graduated to house building in Highbury, Stoke Newington, Bloomsbury, and most famously in Belgravia, where many of London's grandest houses, their opulence undiminished, still testify to his skills. Cubitt had the ability to deal with the aristocracy, who granted him leases to build on their land, and his workers, who respected him for his fair and honest ways. He was a bold innovator; faced with low-lying marshland to build on in Pimlico, he used the top layer of clay to manufacture bricks, then raised the land level by importing colossal quantities of demolition material, rubbish, and soil, some of it dug from the new St Katharine's Dock. The Duke of Westminster, head of the Grosvenor Estate, whose family gained so much wealth through Cubitt's efforts, unveiled this statue in 1995.

Continue for a few yards to the junction with Lupus Street and turn left. Keep on ahead, passing the graceful St Saviour's church, which was also designed by Thomas Cundy and dates from 1864, and one of the few remaining cabmen's shelters, in the characteristic shade of green. Carry on ahead past a pub, café, toilet, and Pimlico station, to continue along Bessborough Street. Follow this road, which leads into Drummond Gate, to meet Vauxhall Bridge Road. Cross straight over at the lights to continue along Causton Street, then take the first right, Ponsonby Place. Cross John Islip Street at the refuge and keep on ahead, passing the Morpeth Arms pub (which serves real-ale), then turn left and walk along Millbank.

Henry Moore's 'Locking Piece'

As you stroll along this wide road, pause to admire the scene to your right, which includes 'Locking Piece', a sculpture by Henry Moore in the foreground, backed by Vauxhall Bridge, the space-age St George's apartment blocks, and the fortress-like, green-windowed MI6 building across the water. On your side of the road is a graceful work of art, 'Jete'.

Carry on ahead past a cul-de-sac to take the next left turn, Atterbury Street, beside Tate Britain.

In 1890 the massive Millbank prison was demolished, providing the perfect site for this British art gallery, which was given to the nation by sugar refiner Sir Henry Tate. In his gift he stipulated that his important art collection should not be housed in one of the major galleries, so in 1897 this handsome building opened, to designs by Sidney RJ Smith, with several new galleries added over the years.

Continue past the shrapnel-scarred walls of the Tate and the stylish buildings of Chelsea College of Art and Design, grouped around a vast parade ground, and then on your right, a fine statue of the painter Millais. Turn left along John Islip Street, then cross with care and take the first right, Cureton Street. Cross two side-streets and then turn right at the T-junction with Causton Street, passing a playground, then go left at Regency Street. Cross over and take the first right, Douglas Street, which continues over Chapter Street to Vincent Square, where you turn right.

This square has been Westminster School's playing field since around 1815, and still regularly exhibits a great deal of enthusiastic sporting activity. It is named after William Vincent, Dean of Westminster Abbey, and previously Head Master of Westminster School, who managed to save this part of Tothill Fields for his pupils' recreation.

Continue round to follow the eastern side of the square, with an appreciative glance along pretty Maunsel Street as you pass, then turn right at Elverton Street, beside the Royal Horticultural Society's Lindley Hall (the 'Old Hall' of 1904), then continue past the 'New Hall' (Lawrence Hall) of 1928 to Horseferry Road. Turn right and then follow this road as it swings left, passing toilets at Regency Place and a medley of interesting architectural styles including the Coroner's Court, Baptist church, a couple of appealing pubs, and a conglomeration of 6 and 7 storey offices. Cross to the left at the traffic lights at Marsham Street (which sports the highly individual Home Office building of 2004, by Terry Farrell & Partners) to maintain your direction on the left-hand pavement (St John's Gardens is opposite, where you can grab a moment of tree-shaded peace), then turn left into Dean Bradley Street, to the church of St John's, Smith Square.

Thomas Archer designed this English Baroque church, which was completed in 1728. The design was not to everyone's liking; over the years it has been unkindly compared to an elephant on its back, also there were rumours that the four towers were built to enable the church to sink evenly (there had been serious problems with the marshy Westminster ground during building). In 1941 the church was burnt out, re-opening as a concert hall in 1969, and thankfully is much more appreciated today for its fine architecture.

Go to the left to make a half-circuit of the square, then turn left into Lord North Street, beside a nameplate announcing 'Smith's Square 1726'. Continue along this delightful early 18th-century street, noting a wartime air-raid shelter sign between numbers 7 and 8, then cross Great Peter Street to Cowley Street, which you follow, passing more original period houses, and a blue plaque to Lord Reith, first Director-General of the BBC. Swing right into Barton Street, where at number 14 TE Lawrence, 'Lawrence of Arabia', is commemorated, and at number 2 these comforting words greet you:

'Peace on Thy House, O Passer By'. Turn left at Great College Street, then at the bend turn right through a gate into Dean's Yard.

In Dean's Yard is the entrance to Westminster School, originally a small charity school founded by the Benedictine monks of Westminster Abbey in 1179. In 1540 the survival of the school was confirmed by statute from Henry VIII, while in 1560 Elizabeth I granted a new charter to 'The College'. The list of 'Old Westminsters' is impressive, and includes Ben Jonson, Christopher Wren, and Charles Wesley, and in more recent times, Andrew Lloyd-Webber, Nick Clegg, and Martha Lane-Fox, to name but a few.

Little Dean's Yard

Walk ahead and then left around the square to leave by the top left-hand corner through an archway which leads you back into the bustle of tourists and traffic, but surrounded by much of interest; opposite is the lavishly-ornamented Methodist Central Hall (which has a good café) and the Queen Elizabeth II Conference Centre (in front of which are public toilets), while on your side of the road are the dramatic 18th-century west towers of Westminster Abbey, and directly in front of you, a tall polished marble war memorial to former Westminster scholars. Turn right past the Abbey shop and continue beside the road towards Parliament Square, to arrive at the entrance to Westminster Abbey, and St Margaret's church.

St Margaret's, Parliament's 'parish church', is a part of Westminster Abbey, and not in the Diocese of London. Famous people who were married here include Samuel Pepys in 1655, John Milton in 1656 (there is a stained glass 'Milton window' in the church), and Winston Churchill in 1908. Sir Walter Raleigh's body was brought here for burial after his execution for treason in 1618, and on the outside of the east wall the bust of another famous figure in history, King Charles I, faces a statue of Oliver Cromwell, a signatory to the King's death warrant, standing outside Westminster Hall. The church contains a rich assortment of memorials going back to the 16th century, and much beautiful stained glass, some of it modern.

Westminster Abbey has been the crowning place of kings and queens since

William the Conqueror claimed the throne here on Christmas Day 1066. The scene as you enter is awe-inspiring; you are immediately surrounded by exquisitely carved marble figures, some larger than life, drawing your eye to the faraway heights of the intricately decorated ceiling. As you tour round the abbey, each new discovery is wonderful; the Coronation Chair; the tomb of Elizabeth I and her sister Mary; the Lady Chapel, which is resplendent with the finest carving and alive with colour and light; and the shrine of St Edward the Confessor. On a lighter note, many famous writers and poets are commemorated in Poet's Corner, including Dr Samuel Johnson, Robert Browning, and Charles Dickens. Two unique features worth looking out for elsewhere in the abbey are a statue of St Matthew wearing spectacles, and England's oldest door, of about 1050.

Cross left at the lights here to continue round Parliament Square and walk past the freshly-restored Supreme Court, formerly the Middlesex Guildhall, which dates from 1913. Across the busy road, figures of the great and the good, mostly with their backs to you, keep a watchful eye on Parliament Square.

Alongside Big Ben are the Houses of Parliament and ancient Westminster Hall, collectively known as the Palace of Westminster since Edward the Confessor built a small palace here in the 11th century so that he could keep an eye on the rebuilding of Westminster Abbey. In 1834 fire destroyed virtually the entire old palace, sparing only the Hall. The new buildings that emerged, designed by Sir Charles Barry, were given their Gothic embellishments by his collaborator, AW Pugin. Between them they produced the most decorative, unique, and spectacular building.

Continue past statues of Abraham Lincoln and George Canning, then cross at the lights and turn right along Great George Street, with Big Ben firmly in your sights, and imposing Government offices of Treasury, Customs and Revenue etc. beside you. In a moment you will arrive at Parliament Street and Westminster station (toilets here), where the walk ends. For Whitehall, Downing Street, and Trafalgar Square turn left, or keep on ahead to Westminster Bridge for all the attractions of the riverside. Buses to all parts leave from the bus stops in Parliament Street.

Westminster Abbey, West Door

Methodist Central Hall

SW1

3 Belgravia

A fine mixture of opulent mansions, extravagant architecture, and lushly-wooded squares, interlaced with cottage-lined mews and traditional, homely taverns

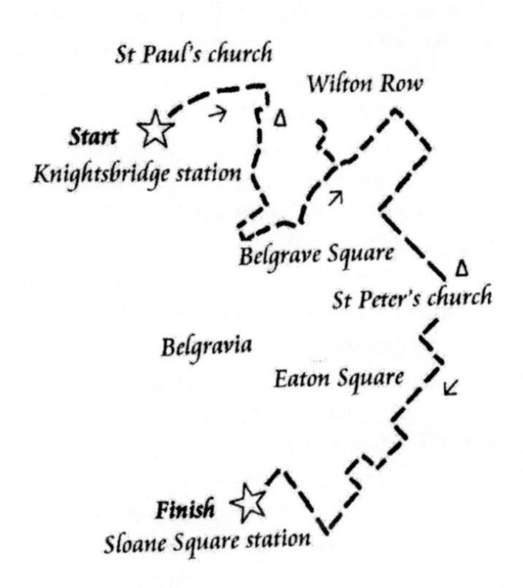

Distance	2¾ miles.
Time	1½-2 hours.
Terrain	Level pavement or tarmac all the way.
Food and drink	Several small pubs and three or four cafés fairly evenly spaced on or very near the route. Duke of York Square, opposite Peter Jones in Sloane Square at the end of the walk has a clutch of popular cafés.
Toilets	Hyde Park Corner (300 yards off route), Sloane Square.
Start	Knightsbridge station. Piccadilly line, Buses 9, 10, 14, 19, 22, 52, 74, 137, 414, 452, C1.
Finish	Sloane Square station. District and Circle lines, Buses 11, 19, 22, 137, 211, 319, 360, 452, C1.

From Knightsbridge station take the exit for Sloane Square and Knightsbridge, then take exit 2 to go straight ahead beside Harvey Nichols. Keep on ahead, crossing Seville Street and William Street.

At this point the Westbourne, one of London's 'lost rivers', used to flow beneath a stone bridge. The story goes that two knights in a company of Crusaders paused here and an argument developed. These two bold warriors, fighting and heavily laden with arms, fell into the river and were drowned, and the locality has been known as Knightsbridge ever since. The Serpentine and Long Water were created from the natural pools and ponds formed by the Westbourne on its way through Hyde Park and Kensington Gardens, but now it has been relegated to a storm culvert, hidden underground. Look carefully and you can still see it through an iron grille, flowing silently deep beneath William Street.

Continue to Wilton Place and turn right, where you will see the church of St Paul's, Knightsbridge, a Gothic design of 1843, with a richly-decorated interior; tiled panels depicting the life of Jesus line the walls, and a beautiful rood screen, and reredos, were added in 1892. Before reaching the church (note plaque to actress Lillie Langtry at number 8) turn right into Kinnerton Street, then turn left opposite the flower-bedecked Wilton Arms. Now you can take your time as you stroll past a delightful medley of pastel cottages, tiny mews entrances, the village store, and The Nag's Head pub, which entices customers with the twin benefits of draught ale and 'no mobiles'. Pass the Knightsbridge car park and a café to the right, tucked away, then turn right at the T-junction with Motcomb Street (Halkin Mews, just to the left, is a charming contrast to all the surrounding opulence, as are all the many little mews and back streets on this walk). Now you pass one or two cafés and the pillared front of the Pantechnicon.

Strangely situated in this high-class locality, the Pantechnicon at first housed a showroom for carriages, a shopping arcade, and an extensive furniture warehouse of Seth-Smith Bros. It was actually built by Seth Smith in 1830 and makes a bold statement with its great Greek Doric columns, but the warehouse section, after being hailed as fireproof, burnt down in 1874.

Turn left at Lowndes Street then left again to follow West Halkin Street, passing Mosimann's Belfry, a private dining club in an intriguing old turret-topped church, formerly a Presbyterian chapel built of Bath stone in 1830. Facing this is Halkin Place and Belgrave Mews West, where real-ale fans can enjoy a pint at The Star Tavern. Carry on to Belgrave Square and turn left to cross Wilton Terrace (just off to the left, Earl Mountbatten of Burma is commemorated with a blue plaque), then follow the north side of the square, passing numbers 10-1, to a statue of Sir Robert Grosvenor.

Belgravia was built on land which Sir Thomas Grosvenor had gained in 1677 on his marriage to heiress Mary Davies, but remained grazing land, intersected by footpaths which divided it into an area known as the Five Fields, until the 1820s when energetic London builder Thomas Cubitt, along with Seth Smith, began the erection on Lord Grosvenor's estate of splendid mansions, squares, and crescents for the wealthy. Belgrave Square was passed on to other developers, who engaged George Basevi to design the majestic stucco houses that line the square, which were built between about 1826 and 1837. Embassies and diplomatic missions, with colourful flags announcing their presence, now occupy many of these mansions, but, less obviously, the sharp-eyed can still spot a peppering of blue plaques in memory of famous past residents. The locality is much smarter now than it was fifty years ago, with landlords the Grosvenor Estate making sure standards don't slip. You may spot a wheatsheaf, the Grosvenor family crest, here and there.

Sir Robert Grosvenor looks out over Belgrave Square

Now the walk diverts briefly to visit a renowned place of refreshment. Turn left into Wilton Crescent and cross to the right-hand side. Turn right into Wilton Row, where you will find The Grenadier, with adjacent sentry-box, just around the corner. The pub is said to be haunted by the ghost of a Grenadier, caught cheating during a card game. Retrace your steps to the statue of Sir Robert, First Marquess of Westminster, where a descriptive plaque tells his story, and how Belgravia got its name. Go across the dual zebra crossing of Grosvenor Crescent, then turn left into Halkin Street to pass more grand buildings, including Forbes House, secluded within its own grounds. Cross the road and at the end turn right to follow busy Grosvenor Place, passing a terrace of colossal mansions sporting marble pillars, wrought-iron balconies, decorous stonework, and melancholy stone faces, oblivious to the thundering traffic, gazing towards the gardens of Buckingham Palace. Take the first right, Chapel Street, an elegant thoroughfare that leads you once more into Belgrave Square, passing Groom Place, which is home to the conveniently-placed Vicolo deli and café, and the Horse and Groom pub. Turn left by the magnificent Seaford House to follow Upper Belgrave Street.

The problem of fitting houses into the corner of a square has been neatly solved here by placing a large mansion diagonally across the corner. Seaford House, built 1842-45 by Thomas Cubitt for the 3rd Earl of Sefton, has a dazzlingly colourful and decorative interior installed in the early 20th century for the 8th Lord Howard de Walden, which is well worth seeing if the house is included in Open House weekend in September. The Royal College of Defence Studies now occupies the building.

Cross Chester Street and then as you pass number 9 look out for a blue plaque to Alfred Lord Tennyson, one of Belgravia's illustrious residents. Soon you arrive at Eaton Square, and the parish church of St Peter.

St Peter's church

St Peter's was Belgravia's first church and opened in 1827. It has twice suffered major fires, in 1836 and again in 1987, but after restoration looks splendid in mellow Bath stone, with its huge portico of Greek Ionic columns, and bright interior. It faces Eaton Square, hardly a square at all as it is about one third of a mile long. The houses here were mostly constructed by Thomas Cubitt, between 1826 and 1855.

Keep straight ahead to cross Hobart Place at the lights, then immediately cross to the right (or keep straight on for a coffee bar and pub at the junction with Ebury Street) and turn left beside the wooded greenery of Eaton Square. Turn right to walk alongside the impressive houses of this most prestigious address, then take the first left into Eccleston Street. Cross with care to the right-hand side, then turn right into Chester Square and continue to Elizabeth Street, passing St Michael's church.

Chester Square enjoys a level of tranquillity sufficient to encourage birdlife such as the blackbird, greenfinch, and robin, whose songs you may be lucky enough to hear, while the square is complemented by St Michael's church, built of Kentish ragstone and dating from 1846. The design is by Thomas Cundy II, surveyor to the Grosvenor estate.

Turn left at Elizabeth Street, cross over and take the first right, Gerald Road, passing the site of the Gerald Road police station (spot the diminutive iron policeman in front) and the former home of Sir Noel Coward, 'Author, Composer and Actor' at number 17. Turn right at South Eaton Place, passing Chantry House, then take the first left to follow Chester Row. By the Duke of Wellington pub turn left into Eaton Terrace, then cross over to take the first right, Graham Terrace, where the houses are much more modest, but still possess a good deal of charm. Continue past St Mary's Bourne Street, built 1873-74, and the handsome red-brick Francis Holland school for girls, then at the junction with Bourne Street (note the quaint little Fox and Hounds, a real-ale pub, ahead), turn right and cross to the left-hand side, where a peep-hole between buildings reveals a bird's-eye view of Sloane Square station and another hint of the hidden Westbourne, this time in a covered duct slanting across the platforms. At the T-junction turn left into Cliveden Place, which quickly brings you to Sloane Square and walk's end.

Eaton Square

Two scenes from Walk 4: 'Isis', by The Serpentine (above), and below, Kensington Palace

SW1, SW7, W2

4 The Serpentine and Kensington Gardens

Endless acres of grass, trees, water, and fresh air, leading to the spectacular Albert Memorial, Albert Hall, and South Kensington Museums

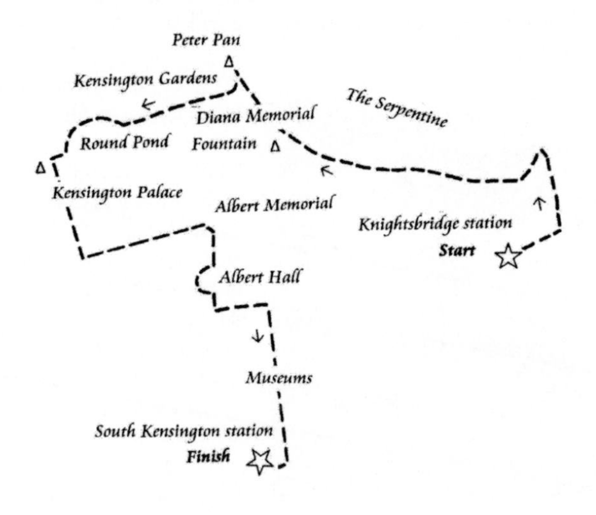

Distance	3¼ miles.
Time	2 hours.
Terrain	Mostly pavements and tarmac paths, with one flight of steps and some soft ground to negotiate, easily avoided by short detours.
Food and drink	Serpentine and Lido cafés, and plenty of choice in South Kensington, especially in Bute Street.
Toilets	Lido, Palace Gate, South Kensington.
Start	Knightsbridge station. Piccadilly line, Buses 9, 10, 14, 19, 22, 52, 74, 137, 414, 452, C1.
Finish	South Kensington station. Circle and District lines, Buses 14, 49, 70, 74, 345, 360, 414, 430, C1.

From Knightsbridge station take the exit for Sloane Street and Knightsbridge, then take exit 2 and walk alongside Harvey Nichols, with the Mandarin Oriental hotel across the road. Cross Seville Street and at the traffic lights at William Street cross to the left to go ahead through Albert Gate into Hyde Park. Cross South Carriage Drive and carry straight on, sharing with a cycle track.

Two old boundary stones here signify the change from SW1 to W2 post-code, while an extra-long drinking trough and a plain mounting block are signs of the proximity of Rotten Row, the 'Route du Roi', a well-trodden horse ride that in bygone days served as the royal way to Kensington Palace.

Cross the sandy horse track and dip down into The Dell, where a gentle cascade feeds a lazy watercourse. Now the path rises, and at the top your walk turns sharp left to cross the waterfall, with the Serpentine (and café) now in view.

The Serpentine

In common with many of London's parks, Hyde Park first rose to prominence as a royal hunting ground. Previously having belonged to the Abbot of Westminster, it fell into the king's hands at the Reformation in the 1530s, becoming another deer-park for Henry VIII to hunt in. One hundred years later it had become a public park, but in 1652 the Commonwealth government sold it to a private owner, a 'sordid fellow' according to diarist John Evelyn, who charged admission. Hyde Park finally became open to all when Charles II regained the throne in 1660. The Serpentine started life as an ornamental adaption of the River Westbourne, which already formed a succession of ponds and lakes on its southward course through the park. In later years it became polluted and by 1860 had been diverted underground, where it still flows to this day. You may notice a small memorial here to Queen Caroline, wife of George II, 'for whom the Long Water and Serpentine were created between 1727-31'.

Turn right to follow the Serpentine's bank, with a playground to your left, all the way to the Lido, which has toilets and a café where you can sip your drink by the lake. Continue past the freely-flowing Diana, Princess of Wales memorial fountain and the gracefully curvaceous Isis statue to stick to the water's edge and walk under the Serpentine Bridge, where you leave Hyde Park and enter Kensington Gardens. Carry on ahead with a railed-off strip of woodland, and the waterside, on your right.

Princess Diana Memorial Fountain

At first reserved for royalty from the time when William III acquired Kensington Palace, Kensington Gardens had by the early 19th century become open to the general public. William and Mary, Queen Anne, and later Queen Caroline, all added more land to the original 26-acre gardens, creating today's pleasant surroundings of lightly-wooded informality, criss-crossed with smooth paths. Your walk includes several fine statues and monuments within the gardens, perhaps the best known being Peter Pan, commissioned by JM Barrie from George Frampton in 1912, much climbed upon by young children, and in 1921 voted London's best statue; Physical Energy by GF Watts, 1904; and the lavishly-decorated Albert Memorial. There is also a youthful Queen Victoria, sculpted by her daughter, Princess Louise.

Soon you meet a path coming in from the left, which will be your route after a short diversion to the statue of Peter Pan. Keep on ahead for 100 yards to see the statue, then retrace your steps to take this path (which will then be to your right) and then turn right again to follow a straight tree-lined path to the statue of Physical Energy, a rather startling figure on horseback. From here maintain your direction by following a sign for Round Pond, with Kensington Palace now firmly in your sights. Follow round to the right to complete a half-circuit of the pond, then turn right to the statue of Queen Victoria, on the Broad Walk.

Peter Pan in Kensington Gardens

At this point the walk turns left, but a 5-minute detour to the right will reveal the Diana, Princess of Wales children's playground, which features amongst other delights a giant sand-pit containing a sailing ship for the young ones to clamber on, and plenty of places to play hide-and-seek and generally romp about. There is also the Elfin Oak, a gnarled tree-trunk from Richmond Park, carved with dozens of cheerful, brightly-coloured elves. Comedian Spike Milligan successfully campaigned for the restoration of this unique treasure in the 1960s.

Turn left on the Broad Walk, usually in the company of a great multitude jogging, cycling, and promenading next to Kensington Palace.

William III, unable because of his asthma to put up with the polluted air and damp surroundings of the royal palaces at St James's and Whitehall, paid 18,000 guineas in 1689 for what was then Nottingham House, then kept Sir Christopher Wren busy with the task of transforming the old house into a royal palace. William died in 1702, after which the palace was occupied by Queen Anne, and later Queen Caroline, both of whom made great improvements to Kensington Gardens and the Serpentine. From the time of George III royalty moved to Buckingham Palace and apart from the birth of Queen

Victoria in 1819, Kensington Palace declined in importance until more recent times when Princess Margaret, and Diana, Princess of Wales, lived here.

Carry on along the Broad Walk, passing St Gover's well, where in the 1870s 'medicinal' water was sold at a penny a glass. Keep going to Palace Gate (where there are toilets) but do not leave the park here, instead turn left through a low iron gate to follow the Flower Walk. Keep on ahead at a crossing path, then at the next gate turn right to the Albert Memorial.

Albert Memorial

The gilded form of Prince Albert, Consort to Queen Victoria, sits comfortably among a superb assortment of carved figures, under a gilt and mosaic canopy, which is surmounted by an intricate, shining spire, rising to 180ft. The Prince Consort was the driving force behind the Great Exhibition, held in Hyde Park in 1851, and the book he holds in his hand is an exhibition catalogue. The memorial, a remarkable work of Victorian skill and artistry, was designed by Sir George Gilbert Scott and completed by 1876.

Descend to cross Kensington Gore to the Albert Hall.

After the highly successful Great Exhibition, Prince Albert suggested using the profits to provide schools, colleges, museums, and a concert hall here, however Albert died in 1861, and it was to be another ten years before the opening of the Royal Albert Hall. It looks circular, but actually measures 272ft by 238ft, with the interior dome reaching 135ft. The annual 'Proms' concerts have been held here since 1941.

Go round to the right of the building, where you will spy the Royal College of Organists, smothered in a type of relief decoration known as sgraffito, and dating from 1876. Bear left to the South Porch (opened by the Queen in 2004) to complete a half-circuit of the Albert Hall, where you will find another fine statue of Albert. Descend a grand flight of steps (to avoid these, turn left, then take the next right turn) to face the Royal College of Music. Cross Prince Consort Road and turn left, passing the Royal School of Mines, a part of Imperial College. At Exhibition Road turn right to walk past the many and varied buildings of Imperial College, and then the Science and Natural History museums, with the Victoria and Albert opposite.

The various museums and seats of learning here were established on land purchased after the Great Exhibition specifically for the purpose. The original museum, known as the 'Brompton Boilers' and made of corrugated iron painted with green and white stripes to give the appearance of a tent, opened in 1857. The Natural History Museum, which features an amazing display of seemingly the entire natural world, was completed in 1881 to designs by Alfred Waterhouse, while the Science Museum, where the explanation of science and technology, and how things work, is totally absorbing for young and old alike, started life in 1928. The Victoria and Albert, designed by Sir Aston Webb and opened by Edward VII in 1909, is considered to be the foremost showcase for applied arts in the country. The tremendous popularity of the museums continues unabated, as you will discover if you attempt a visit at half-term.

On arriving at the busy Cromwell Road you have the choice of using the subway to South Kensington station, where the walk ends, or crossing Cromwell Road and going ahead and then right to find one or two cafés and the Hoop and Toy pub near the station, and a toilet adjacent. 100 yards to the right you will find a multitude of eating places, and the Zetland Arms, in Bute Street.

SW3, SW7

5 Brompton and Knightsbridge

A chance to explore the quaint backwaters and grand terraces of this highly individual locality

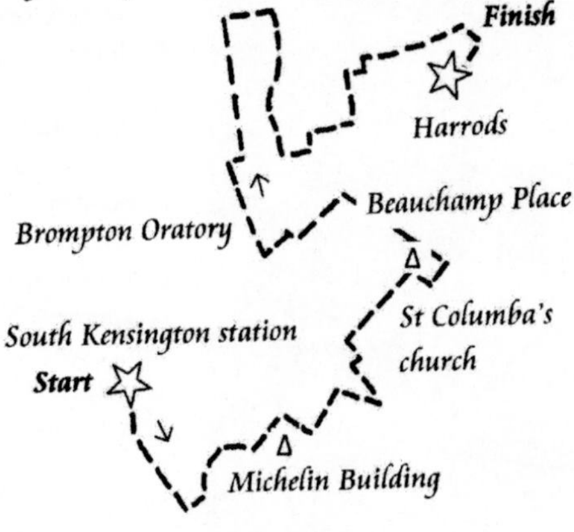

Distance	3 miles.
Time	1½ -2 hours.
Terrain	A few cobbles and a short flight of steps, otherwise fairly level pavements.
Food and drink	Plenty of choice in South Kensington and Knightsbridge.
Toilets	South Kensington.
Start	South Kensington station. Circle and District lines, Buses 14, 49, 70, 74, 345, 360, 414, 430, C1.
Finish	Knightsbridge station. Piccadilly line, Buses 9, 10, 14, 19, 22, 52, 74, 137, 414, 452, C1.

From South Kensington station take the exit for Onslow Square (toilet here), then turn left to cross Pelham Street and carry on along Onslow Square, which continues as Sydney Place. Turn left at Fulham Road and then take the first left along Pelham Crescent, passing Pelham Place.

Pelham Crescent constitutes one of the best examples of the profusion of plaster-rendered stucco terraces that appeared from about 1830 onwards in this area. Later on in the walk you will see, nearer to Knightsbridge, the same style of building enlarged into huge 5-storey mansions, with room for servants, and a mews behind to house the carriage and horses. Pelham Place started life as a humble backwater, at first inhabited almost entirely by cabmen, who might scarcely recognise the smart street that we see today. As the area gained status, so residents of note began to arrive, many of whom are remembered in the scattering of blue plaques along the route.

Michelin Building

Go left on meeting Fulham Road and continue to the traffic lights, where you cross to the Michelin building.

Bibendum, the roly-poly tyre man, features in stained-glass on this flamboyant composition of 1911. This was the British headquarters of the Michelin Tyre Company until 1985 when Michelin left, and Sir Terence Conran opened a restaurant, oyster bar and retail space. It's worth having a look at the exterior as you pass by; after 100 years the audacity of the design is still entertaining, and the tiled depictions of early modes of transport are interesting.

Turn left to cross Sloane Avenue, then take the next on the right, Draycott Avenue. Pass Walton Street and turn left into Donne Place, with a rust-red terracotta-faced building inscribed 'Harrods 1911' opposite. Keep going to the end of this cul-de-sac, which almost has the feel of a seaside town with its colour-washed character cottages, then at the end turn right on Bull's Gardens (which sadly lacks much greenery). Turn left into Richard's Place, then at the end, by number 12, go to the right through a passageway to emerge in First Street. Turn left then right, by the Enterprise pub, to walk along Walton Street. After passing an interesting medley of restaurants and shops turn right into Lennox Gardens. Cross to the left and take the first left turn to walk alongside St Columba's Church of Scotland, with Knightsbridge School opposite.

The Church of Scotland was established in London in 1701, and moved from Covent Garden to Knightsbridge in 1884. The Victorian church, destroyed in the Blitz in 1941, was replaced by the clean lines of the present structure, designed by Sir Edward Maufe, in 1955.

Turn left to pass the front of the church, then cross with great care at the lights to go straight ahead on Beauchamp Place, a thoroughfare full of character and interest, including the Beauchamp pub, many and varied shops and restaurants, and The Map House, which features a fine display of maps and globes. When you meet Brompton Road go left and continue to a set of pedestrian lights, where you cross right to Brompton Square and then turn left towards the Brompton Oratory.

Favoured by artistic and literary types from the time of its construction in the 1820s, the genteel environs of Brompton Square have also been home to a string of actresses, playwrights, and for some reason, comic actors.

Brompton Oratory, the Church of the London Oratory of St Philip Neri, is the second largest catholic church in London, after Westminster Cathedral. St Philip Neri established the first Oratory in Rome in the latter part of the 16th century, and since then Oratories have been established in many parts of the world, the first one in England dating from 1848 in Birmingham. Cardinal Newman, whose statue stands a few yards beyond the church, brought St Philip's Oratory to England at the suggestion of Pope Pius IX. The interior of the church is fabulous. Rich carving and fine marble give an unmistakeably

The Church of the London Oratory

Italian feeling, as intended by its designer Herbert Gribble. Instead of aisles off the 52ft nave there are side chapels, complemented by marble statues of the Apostles, carved by Mazzuoli in the late 17th century, and brought from Siena Cathedral. The church was built between 1880 and 1884, with the dome being added in 1896.

At Cottage Place turn right to follow the tree-lined parallel path. To your right is the red-tiled former Brompton Road station, opened for visitors to the museums but then closed in 1934 through lack of passengers.

Pass Holy Trinity church and churchyard, an ideal picnic spot, with grass, trees, and benches. The path ends at cobbled Ennismore Gardens Mews, where you turn right, go through a grand arch, and turn left to follow Ennismore Gardens. Pass the (locked) gardens and a little further on, set back from the road, the Russian Orthodox church.

Old parish boundary stones near Holy Trinity, Brompton

Built as All Saints church between 1846 and 1849, this church is of a rare Early Christian design, by Lewis Vulliamy. The pewless, candle-lit interior, rich with an aroma of incense, maintains the Orthodox tradition, and services are held in both Russian and English.

Keep on ahead towards Kensington Road and the Prince of Wales Gate, giving access to Hyde Park. If you feel like a break in the park, cross over to go through the gate, where you will find some benches to relax on and an exit further along on the right, opposite the continuation of your walk along Rutland Gate.

The towering form of Knightsbridge Barracks announces the home of the Household Cavalry Mounted Regiment, including 300 officers and soldiers, and nearly as many horses. Their history goes back to 1660 when 80 cavalier gentlemen formed the Life Guards to protect King Charles II. Sir Basil Spence designed the present barracks in the late 1960s, replacing the previous damp and dark Victorian buildings, but retaining the huge stone pediment from the riding school of 1880.

Just before meeting the main road turn right at Prince's Gate, which soon slips out onto Kensington Road, along which you stroll for a few yards to take the next right, Rutland Gate. At the end of this oasis of tranquillity turn left along Rutland Mews East and look for an opening on the right with three steps down to Rutland Street, where you turn left, then left again into Montpelier Walk. Take the first right to follow Montpelier Place, passing the small-scale but appealing German Church, which blends well with the low-rise surroundings. Turn left at the Tea Clipper pub into Montpelier Street. Cross to the right-hand side and continue to the top of Montpelier Square, where you turn right, then left into Trevor Place. Again cross to the right and between numbers 9 and 10 take a passageway which skirts the top of Trevor Square and continues, now signed as Trevor Walk, into Raphael Street. Now the painted cottages give way to a canyon of high buildings as you continue through an arch and turn right into Knightsbridge Green, which has two plane trees but no grass.

There is an old legend concerning the origins of 'Knightsbridge'; a company of Crusading knights, travelling to Fulham Palace to be blessed by the Bishop of London before setting off for the East, stopped at the bridge over the Westbourne (about where Albert Gate is now) when a fierce argument broke out between two knights. Heavily laden, and fighting, they both fell into the river and drowned, and the place has been called Knightsbridge ever since. In later years more dark deeds occurred in this lonely village on the route from London to the West, where a huddle of inns and ale-houses were known to harbour footpads and thieves, who preyed on unprotected travellers. Respectability finally arrived with the tremendous building boom in Queen Victoria's time as cheap artisans' houses were swept away to allow the building of mansion blocks on a grand scale, culminating in the unmistakeable grandeur of Harrods. The firm started life as a humble grocer's shop in 1849, and then expanded over the years through offering impeccable service, and selling 'Everything for Everybody, Everywhere'. The present building dates from 1905.

Cross Brompton Road at the pedestrian lights, turn right, and press on through the window-shopping throng to Harrods. The walk ends here, at Knightsbridge station for Piccadilly line trains, or buses to all parts from the nearby stops.

To be seen on Walk 6: Sloane Square, above, and a sample of the craftsmanship displayed in Cadogan Square, below

SW3

6 Chelsea

The King's Road, Royal Hospital, National Army Museum, and many fine old houses, once home to some of the most famous names from history

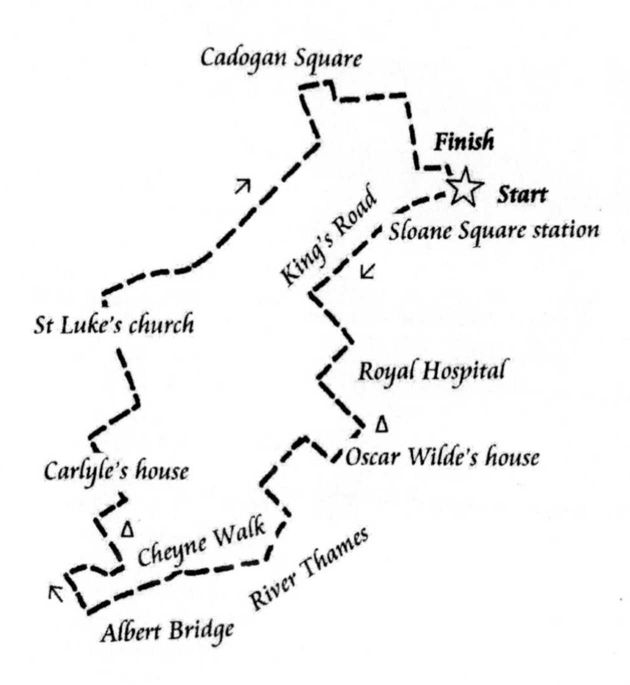

Distance	3½ miles.
Time	2 hours.
Terrain	Level pavements all the way.
Food and drink	Duke of York Square, King's Road.
Toilets	Sloane Square, Chelsea library.
Start and Finish	Sloane Square station. District and Circle lines, Buses 11, 19, 22, 137, 211, 319, 360, 452, C1.

Aim straight ahead from Sloane Square station to walk along the southern side of the square. Cross Lower Sloane Street and carry on to join the King's Road, with Peter Jones department store on your right. Soon you come to Duke of York Square.

Here you can stroll, away from traffic, among shops and pavement cafés. A statue of Sir Hans Sloane, once lord of the manor of Chelsea, overlooks the scene. A few yards further on is a clever reminder, etched into the slabs beneath your feet, that this was once the king's private road, enabling the monarch to enjoy the privilege of this exclusive route by road and water from the royal palace at Whitehall to Hampton Court. The inconvenience suffered by the locals must have been considerable, as the only access to the road, and even this was hard to come by, required the purchase of a token. Eventually in 1830 the King's Road became a public thoroughfare.

Bram Stoker's house

Carry on along King's Road, passing a couple of side turnings, then turn left to follow the wide expanse of Royal Avenue to Burton Court, and a glimpse of the Royal Hospital. Turn right here to follow St Leonard's Terrace, where at number 18, Bram Stoker, author of Dracula, lived. Take the first on the left, Durham Place, which continues as Ormonde Gate, to meet Royal Hospital Road opposite Chelsea Royal Hospital, home of the Chelsea Pensioners.

King Charles II laid the foundation stone of the hospital on the 16th February 1682, and within ten years Sir Christopher Wren's design for a building to house 400 wounded soldiers came to fruition. Little has changed since then apart from some later additions, and the sight of the scarlet-coated pensioners strolling in the central quadrangle known as the Figure Court, the Great Hall, and Chapel, is quite unique. A bronze figure of King Charles by Grinling Gibbons occupies the centre of the quadrangle, and on the King's birthday, 29th May, 'Founders Day' is celebrated, with a parade of the old soldiers around the statue. Entry to the Royal Hospital is free, and there is also a museum, and shop.

Turn right along Royal Hospital Road, passing the National Army Museum (open 7 days 10-5.30, except Bank holidays) then turn right to follow Tite Street (Oscar Wilde's house can be seen by a left turn here). Take the first left into Christchurch Street and keep going to arrive at St Luke's and Christ Church, which dates from 1839. Adding to the charm of this quiet corner of Chelsea is the spruced-up Infant School of 1850.

At the church, follow Christchurch Street round to the left to meet Royal Hospital Road again, with the Chelsea Physic Garden opposite.

The Apothecaries' Company first occupied this site when in 1673 they needed a place to construct a boat house for their ceremonial barge. They also planted a herb garden for medicinal purposes and scientific plant study, which in time became the foremost physic garden in the world. Today the garden has 5000 differently-named plants, and offers garden tours, and a café. It is open Wednesday-Friday and Sunday 1st April-30th October.

Turn right, cross Flood Street, then fork right to stroll along the delightful Cheyne Walk.

Cheyne Walk's mellow old houses, some with sturdy iron railings to match any modern-day security fence, have been home to some famous names over the years. Some merit a blue plaque; George Eliot (actually Mary Ann Evans) author of The Mill on the Floss, then at number 16 the artist Swinburne, who lived for a while in this early 1700s house, the home of Dante Gabriel Rossetti, founder of the Pre-Raphaelite group of artists. Rossetti is remembered with a small fountain in the adjoining gardens. A brilliant but eccentric man, he had his own zoo here, which included owls, a racoon, and a wombat, and in the garden, a bull, peacocks, and a kangaroo. Among other Cheyne Walk residents from the art world were Jacob Epstein, Holman Hunt, Whistler, and Turner (his home can be seen on Walk 8). As you pass the tiny entranceway to Cheyne Mews, look out for a descriptive panel that reveals some of the secrets of Henry VIII's mansion, which stood here.

Carry on ahead to meet Oakley Street (a few yards along, at number 56, is another blue plaque; this time to Scott, Antarctic Explorer). Cross straight over at the lights to pass the enchanting sculpture of Boy with Dolphin, and continue along Cheyne Walk, where a figure of Thomas Carlyle, famous Chelsea resident whose house you will see in a moment, faces the river.

Pass Cheyne Row and Lawrence Street to arrive at Chelsea Old Church, once the centre of the original riverside village. Opening hours are 2-4 Tuesday, Wednesday, and Thursday.

Behind the churchyard railings is the noble tomb of Sir Hans Sloane, physician, local dignitary, and president of the Royal Society, who lived till the ripe old age of 92. His memory is kept alive in a profusion of street, square, and crescent names hereabouts. A sombre, gilded statue of Sir Thomas More, facing the Thames, is a reminder of one of Chelsea's first illustrious residents. He rose to be Henry VIII's Lord Chancellor, and presided over a

Sir Thomas More looks out over Chelsea Embankment

happy household of children and relatives in his fine new mansion before he fell from grace and ended up in the Tower.

Turn right to follow Old Church Street, with Roper's Gardens opposite. After 100 yards take a right turn into Justice Walk, at the end of which you turn right into Lawrence Street, and then opposite the Cross Keys pub turn left into Lordship Place. Turn left again into Cheyne Row to discover Carlyle's house at number 24, which is open March 18th- November 1st, Wednesday-Sunday. The home of the great historian, author of a history of the French Revolution, is now in the care of the National Trust. **Keep on ahead to a junction with Upper Cheyne Row,** by Sir Thomas More Catholic church. Originally the Church of the Holy Redeemer, it was designed by Edward Goldie and opened in 1905. Carry on ahead, following the twists and turns of Glebe Place. After a right-hand bend look for an entrance to 1 and 2 Hans Studios, where a plaque informs the curious passer-by that Charles Rennie Mackintosh, 'Scottish architect and designer of the Glasgow School of Art' and his wife Margaret Macdonald worked here from 1915-23.

Quirky old buildings, and particularly artists' studios, line Glebe Place. Their appeal is underlined by the £17 million price tag of one of the studios that recently went on the market. As you stroll along the street you may also notice a 20th-century folly at number 50, beside the Chelsea Open Air nursery school, a quaint pantiled cottage huddled in a corner of the street. It used to be known as Henry VIII's hunting lodge, although it really is not that old, more probably dating from the 17th century.

Glebe Place ends at the King's Road, where you turn right.

To your right are some interesting old houses; the former homes of actress Ellen Terry, film director Sir Carol Reed, and Argyll House, 18th-century residence of the Duke of Argyll. In the 1920s and 30s this house witnessed many lavish society parties thrown by Lady Sybil Colefax, trying to outdo her neighbour, Mrs Syrie Maugham.

Cross at the pedestrian lights and continue past Chelsea fire station and Dovehouse Green, then turn left along Sydney Street. Opposite you will see the Old Town Hall and Chelsea library, which has toilets on the first floor. Carry on past the farmer's market, then cross over to St Luke's church.

The impressive Gothic revival church of St Luke's comes as quite a surprise in this residential area. Designed by James Savage and costing the huge sum of £40,000 when built in 1819-24, it features flying buttresses and a tower 142ft high, and witnessed the marriage of Charles Dickens and Catherine Hogarth in 1836. Another wedding, this time part of a Disney production of '101 Dalmatians', was filmed here in 1995.

Pass the church and turn right along Cale Street, where you will see an entrance to a playground in the churchyard. Keep on ahead to arrive at a tiny tree-shaded green, where you diverge to the left to follow Whitehead's Grove. Cross Sloane Avenue and press on ahead, now on Cadogan Street.

Quite at odds with today's image of trendy Chelsea, parts of this locality were cramped streets of run-down and overcrowded artisans' dwellings which were swept away, in the face of fierce opposition from the thousands who were evicted, to make room for the mansion blocks that appeared from the 1880s onwards. In later years the Guinness Trust, Samuel Lewis Trust, and the local authority provided more 'affordable housing' for Chelsea's working people.

Pass St Joseph's school, then opposite St Mary's Catholic church turn left to follow Moore Street to arrive at the church of St Simon Zelotes. This ragstone structure of 1859 was designed by Joseph Peacock. With the opulent mansions of Lennox Gardens in view, turn right to follow Milner Street, crossing Clabon Mews, to Cadogan Square. Turn right then first left along the square, noting the former home of novelist Arnold Bennett at number 75. Keep straight on along Cadogan Gate, crossing Pavilion Road, to meet Sloane Street, where you turn right.

Hidden away across the road in Sloane Terrace is the magnificent Cadogan Hall, previously the First Church of Christ Scientist, designed in Byzantine style by R Chisholm. The granite foundation stone came all the way from

Concord, New Hampshire, USA, with the church being completed by 13th June 1909. A little further along Sloane Street is Holy Trinity, designed by John Dando Sedding and completed by 1890, a building that amply displays the 5th Earl of Cadogan's belief that no expense should be spared on the church and its fittings. Inside, bronze, richly coloured marble, alabaster, and stained glass are worked with the finest Arts and Crafts skills to produce a breathtaking spectacle. The Great east window, the largest ever produced by Morris and Co, is a lasting testament to the brilliance of designer Edward Burne-Jones. Everything that the eye lights upon is beautifully crafted.

Sloane Square now beckons, and this is where your walk ends. A little exploration of the square will bear fruit, for apart from Peter Jones, which has an excellent and comfortable café on the top floor, there is the Royal Court theatre, and in the centre of the square a fountain with a relief depicting King Charles II being tempted by Nell Gwynne. As a final thought, if you are catching the Tube from Sloane Square station, look up to see a gently-sloping cast iron aqueduct crossing tracks and platforms, marking the course of the Westbourne, one of London's 'lost rivers'.

Holy Trinity, Sloane Square

SW5

7 Earl's Court

An exploration of some of the grand squares, fine houses, and hidden corners in one of London's most cosmopolitan districts

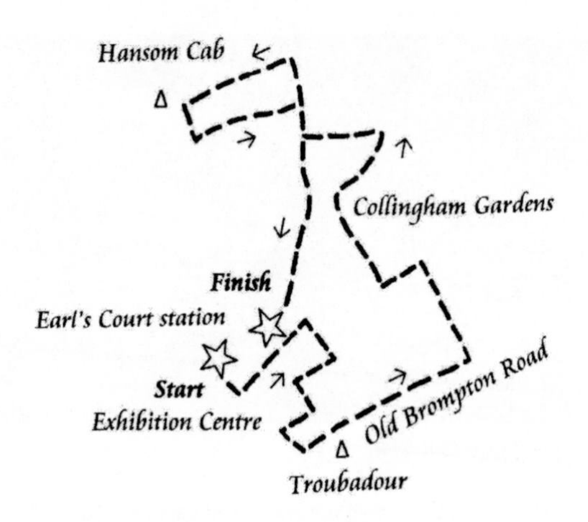

Distance	2¾ miles.
Time	1½ hours.
Terrain	Level pavements all the way.
Food and drink	numerous pubs, cafés, and restaurants in Earl's Court, including the Troubadour and the King's Head.
Toilets	Earl's Court station main concourse.
Start and Finish	Earl's Court station. District and Piccadilly lines, Buses C1, C3, 74,328.

From the station, take the exit for Exhibition and Warwick Road and, facing the exhibition halls, turn left into Warwick Road.

From William the Conqueror's day the De Vere family had been lords of the manor of Kensington, while Earl Aubrey De Vere achieved high office as Lord Chief Justice of England. The family seat, known as Earl's Court manor house, soon lent its name to the area. Sparsely populated, but increasingly known for its market gardens, the advent of the District Railway in the 1870s sparked a sequence of grand housing developments for the better-off. Eventually Earl's Court became known for entertainments and events, hosting the American Exhibition of 1887. The year 1894 saw the erection of the Great Wheel, a precursor of the London Eye, which took 20 minutes to complete its circuit. Once it became stuck, forcing all the passengers to spend the night aloft, resulting in £5 compensation each when release finally came the next morning. In 1895 the Empress Theatre, named after the Empire of India exhibition of that year, opened its doors. Requisitioned by the government in the First World War and then lying unused for many years, the exhibition grounds sprang back to life in 1937 when the current halls opened.

Earl's Court exhibition centre

Take the first left, Penywern Road, and carry on to meet Earl's Court Road where you turn right, then take the next right into Earl's Court Square. On reaching the garden square turn left, passing Farnell Mews.

After years of neglect the gardens here were given a new lease of life in the 1970s, a century after the square was first laid out, with the help of a local garden designer and the newly-formed residents' association. The surrounding mansions, that give the square such character, are a rich mixture of Italianate, and on the south side, red-brick Flemish styles, and look much smarter now than in the 1960s and 70s when a profusion of run-down bedsits in 'Kangaroo Valley' were home to a growing band of Australians and New Zealanders attracted by the bargain accommodation.

Cross over and turn right at the end of the square to walk alongside the stylish red-brick houses and the ornate entrance to Langham Mansions. At Warwick Road turn left, then left again at Old Brompton Road, with the famous Troubadour opposite.

Memories of a thousand nights of live music and conviviality greet you as you enter the Troubadour; hosting informal folk music sessions since 1954, the relaxingly rustic interior has accommodated such names as Bob Dylan, Jimi Hendrix, and Joni Mitchell, and continues this proud tradition today with more live music, poetry readings, and as an added extra, wine tastings. Don't be put off by all this excitement though; you can still pop in for a coffee and snack, enjoyed in the vine-draped garden, weather permitting. Coleherne Court, the nearby mansion block, can boast several famous past residents including in their younger days Diana, Princess of Wales, and Sophie Rhys-Jones, Countess of Wessex. Earl's Court is also distinguished as the birthplace of architect Sir Edwin Lutyens, archaeologist Howard Carter, and perhaps most famously Beatrix Potter, at number 2 The Boltons.

Inside the Troubadour

Keep on ahead across Earl's Court Road and past Brompton Library to a set of traffic lights, where you turn left into Bolton Gardens. Carry on ahead to follow Collingham Gardens, which abounds with fine examples of the bricklayer's art.

Reserved for residents only, the gathering of garden squares encountered on this walk enhance the surroundings to such an extent that they often feature in the annual Open Garden Squares weekend, when the public are welcome to enjoy these verdant reminders of Victorian good taste. Collingham Gardens is home to some unique and individual houses, designed by Ernest George and Harold Peto in a Flemish Gothic style and built between 1881 and 1888. Grade II listed, they are grouped around an informal planting of trees and shrubs in a square which still sports its original entrance gate. Collingham, a village in West Yorkshire, referred to the country estate of Robert Gunter, whose profitable market-gardens in Earl's Court became an irresistible development opportunity as land values rose in the mid 1800s. He also ran a successful catering and confectionery business in Berkeley Square.

At a mini-roundabout keep forging on ahead, now on Collingham Road. St Jude's church, built in 1870, stands proudly at the next junction, where you turn left to follow Courtfield Gardens. Turn right at the end of this square and keep on ahead, using a zebra crossing to gain the right-hand pavement, to pass a modern hotel in what is now Knaresborough Place. Soon you meet the main artery of Cromwell Road where you cross at the pedestrian lights, turn right for a few yards then left into Lexham Gardens. Carry on past Pennant Mews, then follow the pavement to the left (or if you wish to explore a surprising cluster of pretty mews cottages, cross the road and look right). At the end of the gardens go over to the right-hand side and turn right along Marloes Road. Use the zebra crossing by the Devonshire Arms to continue on the left-hand pavement, then take the next left turn, Scarsdale Villas. Follow this leafy road to its end, on the way passing St Mark's church on the corner of Allen Street, and then Abingdon Road.

Facing you as you meet Earl's Court Road is Pembroke Square, flanked with modest but appealing Georgian terraces built around 1800, and fronted by Rassell's long-established garden centre. Completing this attractive scene is the Hansom Cab, which since 1810 has recalled the inventor of that fine machine, local resident Joseph Hansom. Until about 10 years ago an actual cab, hanging, occupied the back bar; sometimes over-boisterous drinkers would climb into it, resulting in it being deemed a health hazard. On its removal, it was found to be the genuine article, and now graces a museum.

Turn left to follow Earl's Court Road, then take Stratford Road, the first left turn, with St Philip's church on the corner. As you stroll along look out for Sunningdale Gardens, a little, hidden, emerald-green enclave of dwellings. Press on past a collection of well-kept mews and side turnings amongst a parade of useful shops, to meet Marloes Road again at the Devonshire Arms. Turn right and carry on to meet the busy Cromwell Road once more, where you cross at the lights (when you are safely across, glance up at the house straight ahead to spy a blue plaque in memory of famous composer Benjamin Britten). Turn left for a very few yards, and then turn right into Kenway Road. Continue along this charming street of old cottages and shops, then keep left of the King's Head to follow Hogarth Place, which leads through to Hogarth Road. Carry on the short distance to the end of this road, which will bring you to Earl's Court station and walk's end.

The Hansom Cab

SW3, SW10

8 Walham Green and World's End

The rustic and peaceful Brompton Cemetery, a superb riverside panorama, glittering King's Road antique shops, and a top-notch playground

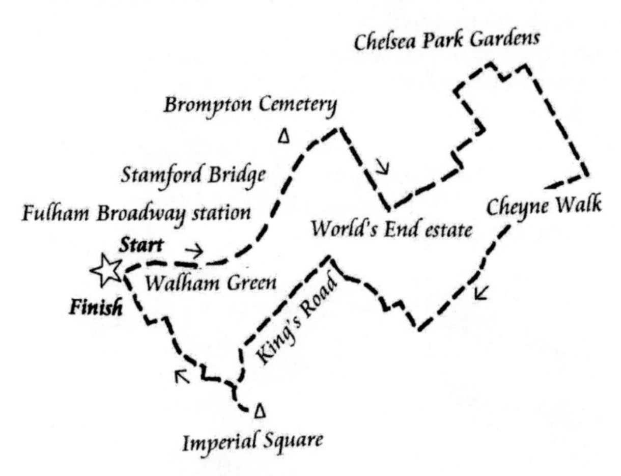

Distance	3½ miles.
Time	1½-2 hours.
Terrain	Pavements, with just a few cobbles to negotiate. Several busy roads to cross, all on pedestrian crossings.
Food and drink	Fulham Broadway and World's End. There are a few cafés, and about ten pubs, intermittently spaced along the route.
Toilets	Cremorne Gardens, Westfield Park.
Start and Finish	Fulham Broadway station. District line, Buses 11, 14, 28, 211, 295, 391, 414, 424.

As you emerge from the shopping mall at Fulham Broadway station, pause for a moment to admire the impressive façade of the Town Hall, which dates from 1890, and then turn left to commence your walk along Fulham Road. Pass the Sir Oswald Stoll Foundation disabled ex-servicemens' flats, soon after which your eye is drawn to the massive outlines of Stamford Bridge, home of Chelsea Football Club.

Founded in 1905, Chelsea had their first big success in 1955, when they were League champions. They won the FA Cup in 1970, and the UEFA Cup Winners' Cup in 1971 and 1972, but the next decade saw limited success and financial problems which led to the club being sold for £1 in 1982. In the 1990s, and by now in the Premier League, their fortunes improved, with an FA Cup win in 1997 followed by more trophies in the next few years. As a testament to the success achieved in twenty years, Russian oil magnate Roman Abramovich paid £140 million for the club in 2003, during a highly successful decade for Chelsea.

Keep on past the walled seclusion of Chelsea Studios, the 'Italian Village', to cross a railway bridge. Note the 1860s boundary markers denoting Fulham parish and St Luke's Chelsea set into the wall here. Carry on past Billing Road, where you will spy trim and colourful cottages alongside the Fox and Pheasant pub. Pass St Mark's Grove, opposite which is the well-restored St Mark's College Chapel, and continue past a terrace of Georgian houses to arrive at the gates of Brompton Cemetery.

Assembled angels in Brompton Cemetery

In company with cemeteries at Nunhead and Highgate, Brompton opened as a commercial venture in 1840 to relieve the overcrowded City churchyards. Formerly market gardens and a brickfield, the half-mile long site exhibits the layout of a cathedral, with architecture to match, and is full of wildlife. The mellow Bath stone domed Anglican Chapel, Colonnades, and catacombs, together with the Central Avenue with its mature limes, and the general air of tranquillity make Brompton Cemetery a very pleasant place to while away an hour or two, or to take advantage of one of the regular guided tours.

Carry on along Fulham Road and cross with care at the traffic lights to continue on the right-hand side, crossing Gunter Grove. Take the next right turn, Fernshaw Road, which you follow to its end to meet the King's Road. Turn left and press on ahead, passing the flamboyant and distinctive World's End Distillery, backed by the raw brown-brick towers and blocks of the World's End estate.

Before the building boom of the 19th century this must have felt like the end of the world, nearing the lonely Thames foreshore after leaving the fields of Chelsea behind. The present World's End pub is the third on this site, having been built in 1897, and thankfully was spared when four surrounding streets and a parade of shops were razed to the ground in the 1960s to clear the site for construction of the World's End estate.

World's End Distillery

After the pub, take the next left into Shalcomb Street, then first right along Lamont Road. Take the second left to follow Limerston Street, then first right at The Sporting Page into Camera Place. Cross Park Walk, home of the fine church of St Andrew's, to enter the verdant environs of Chelsea Park Gardens. You are now in the exclusive SW3 postcode.

St Andrew's church is said to be a good example of Decorated Gothic, and was consecrated in 1913. It towers above the between-the-wars houses of Chelsea Park Gardens, grouped around a central garden square, which occupy ground where, in 1718, two thousand mulberry trees had been planted as a commercial silk-producing venture. The scheme was not a success, but apparently one or two of these old trees are still alive, and the memory lingers on in Mulberry Walk, a street nearby.

Take the first right and follow the road through this miniature garden suburb as it swings left to meet Beaufort Street, where you turn right. Note the blue plaque to Sir Alfred Munnings, president of the Royal Academy 1944-59. Cross King's Road to continue ahead on Beaufort Street, the road leading to the Thames and Battersea Bridge. Turn right before the bridge to follow Cheyne Walk along the riverside.

Screened from public view, the fine residences of Cheyne Walk have housed many famous occupants, as the profusion of blue plaques testifies. Whistler (whose statue graces the riverbank nearby), Marc Brunel and his son Isambard Kingdom Brunel, Hilaire Belloc, JMW Turner at number 119, and Sylvia Pankhurst are among those that have resided in this once-peaceful Thames-side location.

After passing Blantyre Street go across the zebra crossing to continue with the river and a collection of houseboats on your left, to Old Ferry Wharf, where you fork left along Lots Road. Walk through a gate on the left into Cremorne Gardens, which has toilets, a kayaking centre, and a sweeping view of the Thames, looking directly over to the old church of St Mary, Battersea.

Restored original gate in Cremorne Gardens

The twelve-acre Cremorne Gardens were opened in 1845, offering eager visitors to these pleasure grounds a concert room, theatre, maze, circus, and a dance floor with space for two thousand couples. Coloured lights, fountains, and grottoes heightened the romantic appeal, while diners could enjoy seclusion in their own box. Firework displays, balloon ascents, pageants and tournaments added to the lure of the gardens, which could be reached by the King's Road, or a threepenny steamer that sailed from the City to Cremorne Pier. By 1875 Cremorne had become loud and disreputable, and had to close, but fortunately this riverside fragment remains, with its intricate recently-restored iron gateway. The view from here includes the two Battersea bridges (road and rail) and the Belvedere tower at Chelsea Harbour, which is almost a self-contained town, built on 20 acres of land left derelict after the old riverside industries closed.

Leave the gardens and turn left along Lots Road, passing the pumping station of Thames Water, boldly lettered 'London County Council'. The great bulk of the former Lots Road power station now fills the forward view.

Built by the Metropolitan District Electric Traction Co after their decision to change from steam to electric trains, Lots Road power station opened in 1905 and in company with another generating plant at Greenwich provided much of the electricity required for the Underground system. Originally designed to burn coal, and consuming 800 tons per day, with four chimneys belching smoke over Chelsea, Lots Road was converted to oil burning in 1963, leading to demolition of two of the 275ft tall chimneys. Nowadays power for the Underground trains is provided by the National Grid, after Lots Road, having come to the end of its useful life, closed in 2002. There are now major plans afoot to develop the site with a mixture of residential, shops, and restaurants, and two lofty towers, all originally schemed for completion around 2013.

Continue along Lots Road with the power station alongside, and after passing some old industrial buildings at number 90, turn right into Uverdale Road. Take the first left, Burnaby Street, where you can pop into the Chelsea Ram for a pint of real ale if time permits. Turn first right into Upcerne Road to enter Westfield Park, which has toilets in the building on the right, and an elaborate children's playground. Opposite the playground turn left and then right to leave the park and follow Tetcott Road past the green-painted Furniture Cave. Turn left to follow King's Road, where you will see across the road the freshly-revamped buildings of the former St Mark's College, opened in 1840 as a teacher training college, converted in the First World War to a hospital, then later reincarnated as a university campus. Carry on over a railway bridge (more boundary markers here), then continue past a collection of up-market antique and interior shops, the Imperial Arms, and a petrol filling station, and then turn left at the Hand and Flower pub into Edith Row, where motorbike fans will appreciate Warr's, 'Europe's oldest Harley dealership', which sports a mouth-watering display of these fine machines. Turn right into Michael Road, with the gas works in view, to a roundabout where there is yet another pub, The Rose, and on your side of the road the Gasworks restaurant on the corner of Waterford Road, resplendent with a selection of rustic carvings and embellishments. At this point, cross over to the left-hand pavement of Harwood Terrace, where you will find a passageway between house numbers 9 and 11 leading to Imperial Square.

This secret enclave of terraced cottages started life as housing for workers at the Imperial Gas Company's works, being so close to the gigantic gasholders as to offer little excuse for ever turning up late for work. The square was built in 1880, and renovated a century later. It was sometimes called 'German Square', after a contingent of Germans and Russians kept the gasworks operating during a strike, and were housed here.

After visiting the square, retrace your steps and turn left to follow Waterford Road, crossing King's Road at the pedestrian lights a few yards to your left, then turning by The Morrison pub. At the first road junction turn left along Moore Park Road, with the Pelican pub on the corner, and a cigar shop opposite. Take the first right, Cedarne Road, which will take you directly to the end of the walk at Fulham Broadway station.

Chelsea Harbour

SW6

9 Fulham

A treasure-trove of children's delights at Bishop's Park, plus historic Fulham Palace, and the traditional market stalls of North End Road

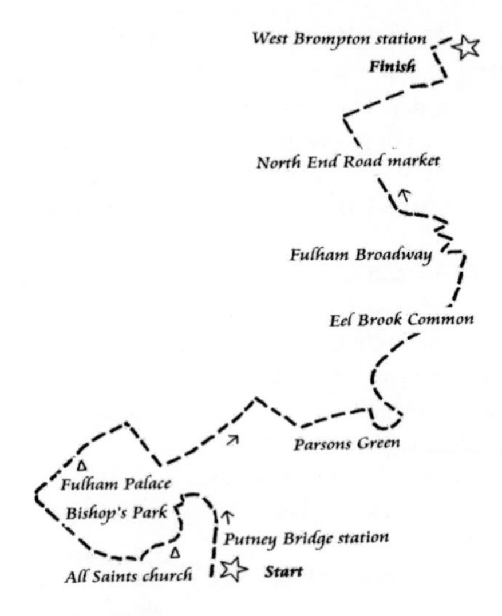

Distance	4 miles.
Time	2½ hours.
Terrain	Level pavements and tarmac paths.
Food and drink	Two cafés in Bishop's Park, Coffee and Crayons in Fulham Road, two or three pubs and the Peterborough café at Parson's Green, and a wide choice in Jerdan Place and North End Road.
Toilets	Bishop's Park, Vanston Place, West Brompton.
Start	Putney Bridge station. District line, Buses 14, 22, 39, 74, 85, 93, 220, 265, 270, 414, 424, 430.
Finish	West Brompton station. District line and Overground trains to Clapham Junction, Shepherd's Bush etc. Buses 74, 430.

Turn right on leaving Putney Bridge station to walk along a wide passageway beside the railway arches. This leads to New King's Road, where you cross with care at the refuge and turn right, then first left into Burlington Road, by the old bottle kiln of the Fulham Pottery.

This shapely old structure marks the site of a venture established by John Dwight in 1671. He produced stoneware and transparent earthenware, and his statuettes and busts were considered to be the finest examples of white salt-glaze, one of which, of his little daughter Lydia, is at the Victoria and Albert museum. The pottery had its ups and downs over the next 200 years, at one point being declared bankrupt, but in 1891 George Cheavin bought the business and turned its fortunes around with the manufacture of water filters, and during the First World War, hot water bottles and rum jars for the troops. At the height of demand nine coal-fired kilns were in use. Later years saw the production of much art pottery, followed by a move to Battersea.

Follow this road, passing Dwight House, then take the first on the left, Rigault Road. Turn left at Fulham High Street, cross at the crossing and continue on the right-hand pavement to turn right at the Temperance pub into Church Gate.

Apart from numbers 5 and 6, two 17th-century houses, Church Gate is also home to Sir William Powell's almshouses. They were first established in Burlington Road in 1680, rebuilt in 1792, then moved here in 1869. These twelve little Gothic cottages are graced with a turret and outer staircase, with carved heads of Faith, Hope, and Charity, and little figures of Miriam, Anna, Deborah, Dorcas, Ruth, and St Mary.

Keep on ahead through the churchyard of All Saints, and past the church door, which has an inner glass door allowing you to 'Pause, Look and Pray'.

First mentioned in 1154, the oldest part of the church now is the early 15th-century tower, the remainder having been rebuilt 1880-81 by Sir Arthur Blomfield, son of the Bishop of London. Many interesting monuments from the old church still exist, including a fine Flemish brass of 1529 to Margaret Saunders, discovered during work on the foundations in 1770. The organ and font date from the 17th century. Several Bishops of London, and two Lord Mayors, are buried in the churchyard, which also contains an amusing epitaph to Isobella and Joseph Murr.

Leave the churchyard and turn right to enter the gates of Bishop's Park, by Pryors Bank café. Shortly you will see a sign for the Moat Trail, which you will be following. Turn left to the riverside to follow the old course of the moat, long since filled in, which encircled Fulham Palace. This was said to be England's largest medieval moat, in existence since at least the 14th century, and levelled with builders' rubble in the 1920s because it was too expensive to clean it out. Carry on along the riverside, passing a memorial to volunteers of the International Brigade who fought in Spain 1936-39.At the end of the accompanying wide strip of grass, lined with mature plane trees, turn right to Bishop's Avenue and the entrance to Fulham Palace. Here you will find on the left several attractions; a café and toilets, and also a large playground, paddling pool, and sandpit.

The Bishop's Palace is Fulham's oldest building, and the oldest part is the courtyard built by Bishop Fitzjames c1510-20. For 1200 years this has been the country retreat for the Bishops of London, broken only by a short Cromwellian interlude, and over 50 bishops have resided here. They include Bishop Bonner, known for sending many heretics to the stake; Bishop Laud, a high Churchman who supported Charles I and was himself executed in 1645; and Bishop Jackson, who gave Bishop's Park, which opened in 1893, to the people of Fulham.You can get the full story by visiting the museum, after which a stroll round the gardens, and a break in the café, is recommended. Music and craft workshops for children also feature here.

Putney Bridge from Bishop's Park

Follow Bishop's Avenue, with allotments to the right and a bowling green and tennis courts on the left, then pass a school, after which you turn right to walk the final shrub-lined stage of the Moat Trail. Soon your path curves left to leave the park, where you cross at the zebra crossing, and then go right and straightaway left to follow Fulham Road. Use the zebra crossing to continue on the right-hand pavement, passing a Fulham parish milepost which announces 'London 3½, Richmond 4½', soon after which you

The Bishop's Palace

come to Coffee and Crayons, a popular meeting place for young mums, where little ones can enjoy a play area, and various arts and crafts. Turn right at the traffic lights to follow Munster Road, and then use the zebra crossing to continue under the bridge on the left-hand side. Take the first left, St Dionis Road, a street lined with cosy little cottages, ending at red-brick St Dionis' church.

The church of St Dionis, designed by Ewan Christian and completed by 1886, has a 17th-century pulpit, font, and altar from St Dionis Backchurch, one of Sir Christopher Wren's City churches. Located in Fenchurch Street in the heart of the City, it had the distinction of being one of the first churches to be rebuilt after the Great Fire in 1666, but by 1878 was considered redundant, and pulled down.

Turn right at Parson's Green, past a rather superior terrace of Victorian houses sporting wrought-iron balconies and pillared doorways. Cross to the left at the junction with New King's Road to walk alongside the green.

Here you have a good vantage point to view the 18th-century terrace opposite; the individually-named houses are survivors of the days when Parson's Green was just a village, before streets of Victorian houses filled the fields and market gardens between here and Walham Green, North End, and the old high street of Fulham, by the bridge. The Duke on the Green pub occupies the corner of Peterborough Road, where the Peterborough café, a few yards along, used to take orders by name rather than giving each customer a number; this produced some confusion when a fry-up for Mick, or Bill, or John was announced, and half-a-dozen responses came.

Opposite Peterborough Road, take the path heading diagonally right across the green, then cross the road and turn left to pass the fine old buildings of Lady Margaret school. Pass the White Horse pub, cross Ackmar Road, then turn right just before the railway bridge on Novello Street. At Eel Brook Common fork left alongside the railway.

Opened as a public space in 1881, Eel Brook Common had previously been a boggy piece of grazing land, around which a drainage ditch had been dug, said to contain plenty of fish, and of course eels. Nowadays the attractions include two playgrounds, and a fenced sport and play area.

Eventually your path emerges in Erin Close, then after a few yards you meet Effie Road and turn left. Pass Barclay Hall, opposite which is a former Welsh chapel of 1897, then turn right at Barclay Road, and right again at Fulham Road. Cross left at the pedestrian lights to fork left along Jerdan Place, among a choice of pavement cafés, to St John's church.

Situated at the centre of the old village of Walham Green, St John's dates from 1828, and displays an early Gothic revival design, by JH Taylor. The diminutive churchyard accommodated over 500 burials before closure in 1853.

St John's church

Walk past the church (toilets to the right in Vanston Place) with the parish hall and public baths, of 1911 and 1902 respectively, across the road. Now your route follows North End Road for ¼ mile, among a cheerful medley of shops, stalls, and the jostle and aromas of a busy market street that has been attracting customers for well over a century. Just by a zebra crossing, before meeting Lillie Road, turn right to follow Sedlescombe Road. Keep on to the end, then cross Ongar Road to continue on Merrington Road. Turn left at Seagrave Road, cross to The Atlas pub (toilets in car park entrance here) and carry on to Lillie Road, with the bulky form of Earl's Court Two, contrasting with the lofty, 22-storey Empress State building, in view. Turn right here, with two pubs and a café to choose from, to cross the bridge (which has two very old parish boundary markers in the crumbling wall on the left) and find yourself at West Brompton station, where the walk ends. Just a few steps ahead is Brompton Cemetery, which offers a tempting, green respite from your walking endeavours in the midst of an extraordinary collection of Victorian memorials.

North End Road market

SW15, SW18

10 Putney Bridge and Wandsworth

A short but fascinating riverside walk along Thames and Wandle, on a route packed with interest and variety

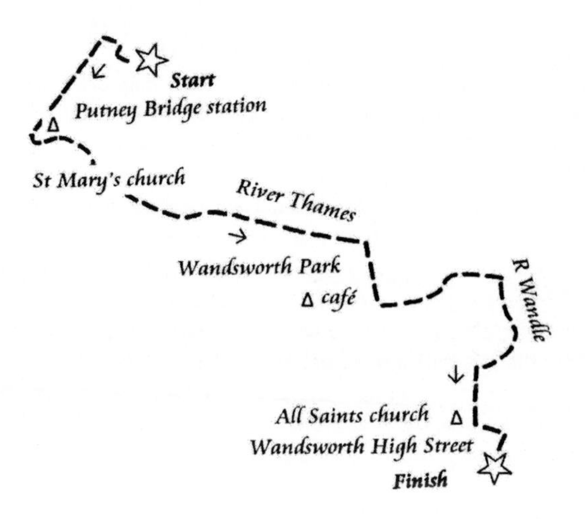

Distance	2½ miles.
Time	1-1½ hours.
Terrain	Fairly level paving or tarmac.
Food and drink	Putney and Wandsworth offer plenty of cafés and pubs, and there is a café in Wandsworth Park.
Toilets	Putney and Wandsworth.
Start	Putney Bridge station. District line, Buses 14, 22, 39, 74, 85, 93, 220, 265, 270, 414, 424, 430.
Finish	Wandsworth town centre. Buses 28, 37, 39, 44, 77, 87, 156, 170, 220, 270, 337, 485 stop at various central points. Wandsworth Town station, for trains to Clapham Junction, Putney etc. is a ten minute walk.

Bear left from Putney Bridge station across the yellow-striped crossing and then fork right along Ranelagh Gardens. Turn right to pass the Eight Bells pub, opposite which you cross with care to turn left into Gonville Street, with the handsome church of All Saints Fulham in view. Turn left to cross Putney Bridge and arrive at St Mary's church.

During the Civil War this handsome church with its 15th-century tower was the scene of the 1647 Putney Debates, where calls for greater democracy and equality from officers within Oliver Cromwell's army, known as the 'Levellers', were too much for Cromwell, who quickly re-asserted his authoritarian regime. Now much more peaceful, the church often hosts orchestral concerts, and has the added attraction of Sally's café (with customer toilet). In Cromwell's day there was no bridge across the Thames here; the first bridge, of wood, appeared in 1729, being replaced by the present elegant structure in 1886, designed by Sir Joseph Bazalgette.

Turn left into Church Square and pass a war memorial, to arrive at the riverside by the distinctive bulk of Putney Wharf. Continue past the Boathouse pub and a pavement café to leave the river and emerge onto Deodar Road. Turn left and continue to the end.

Originally built for the London & South-Western Railway, the iron-lattice bridge here carries the District line, and a footbridge, across the Thames to Putney Bridge station. Deodar Road has the highly desirable and unusual feature of houses with gardens that lead right down to the riverbank.

Go straight ahead through Blade Mews into Wandsworth Park, and then follow the riverside row of noble London plane trees. At the far end of the park, near the playground, is the excellent Culture Café, offering home-cooked food seven days a week from 10am (and customer toilet), and there is also a toilet nearby in Putney Bridge Road.

Riverside scene from Wandsworth Park

Before being opened in 1903, Wandsworth Park had been an area of market gardens, and one of the borough's last undeveloped riverside sites. Nowadays it offers a much-needed green space among so many bulky blocks of flats on the riverbank, its greenery matched on the far bank by the genteel, tree-clad opulence of the Hurlingham Club.

Continue along by the Thames and out of the park, passing a cluster of king-size houseboats. Turn right into Point Pleasant, past an iron sculpture, and carry on past the Cat's Back pub (the name, apparently, simply refers to an errant feline that returned). Just before a railway bridge, turn left opposite Prospect Cottages into Osiers Road. After a left-hand bend cross to follow Enterprise Way, and keep on ahead to bridge the Wandle.

Point Pleasant sculpture

Once described as the hardest-worked river in the world, this fast-flowing watercourse rises in Waddon and Carshalton and then falls over 100ft in its 9½ mile length. Thirteen watermills were recorded in the Domesday survey, and in later years up to 90 mills were engaged in producing flour, snuff, oil, paper, copper, iron, and from 1881 included William Morris's famous printing works at Merton Abbey. One mill even squeezed, from brazil wood, a red dye that was used to colour locally-made hats for the clergy in Rome. The Surrey Iron Railway, renowned as the first public railway in the world, ran horse-drawn wagons from a wharf here all the way to Merstham between 1803-46. There are a few relics of the railway displayed in the brewery wall in nearby Ram Street.

When you are across the first of two river channels turn right on a brick-paved path, through an arch, to follow the Wandle along The Causeway.

This quickly brings you to two of Wandsworth's many historic buildings; The Armoury, previously named The Crane, one of the town's oldest pubs, and 18th-century Wentworth House, former home of engineers Wentworth and Sons, a few yards along Dormay Street.

Go past The Armoury and a row of old houses, cross Frogmore, then cross Armoury Way at the lights to go ahead on Wandsworth Plain.

Church Row, Wandsworth Plain

Soon you come across Church Row on the left, sporting a sundial of 1723, although numbers 1-6 were erected in 1718. Built of brick with three storeys, they originally had gardens leading down to the Wandle. To your right is All Saints church, with a tower built in 1630 and various later additions, and a fine interior containing carved woodwork, stained glass, and ancient monuments to local worthies. There has been a church on this site since at least the 13th century.

Cross left at the lights, then right at the next set of lights on the High Street, just before the River Wandle bridge, to the end of this walk at Southside shopping centre. Buses to all parts stop here, also further up the High Street opposite the Town Hall, and in Garratt Lane. A signposted walk of no more than ten minutes will lead you to Wandsworth Town station.

SW15

11 Roehampton and Putney

A surprisingly traffic-free walk revealing some very pleasant hidden attractions of this historic locality

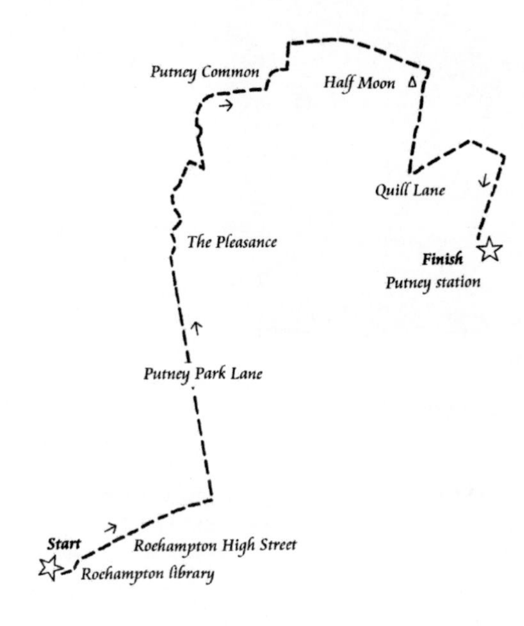

Distance	3½ miles.
Time	1½-2 hours.
Terrain	One long and uneven gravel lane, and a railway foot-bridge, otherwise fairly level pavements and tarmac.
Food and drink	One or two pubs and cafés in Roehampton, and plenty of choice in Putney.
Toilets	Roehampton, Putney.
Start	Roehampton library. Buses 85, 170, 430, 493.
Finish	Putney station. Trains to Clapham Junction, Barnes etc. Buses 14, 37, 39, 85, 93, 337, 424, 430.

Start from the library in Danebury Avenue, cross Roehampton Lane at the lights and go straight ahead up the High Street.

Blackford's Passage

In the 18th and 19th centuries Roehampton and Putney were renowned for the fine villas that graced this rural locality next to Richmond Park. Designed by such famous names as Thomas Archer and James Wyatt, with Capability Brown adding some of the garden splendour, many of these grand buildings are still with us, having been incorporated into more recent building schemes and local institutions.

Roehampton today is dominated by the Alton estate. Alton East appeared in the early 1950s and has over 700 dwellings covering nearly 30 acres; Alton West came a few years later, with almost 1900 dwellings on 100 acres. Reckoned to be of some architectural merit, these tall blocks certainly provide superb views over Richmond Park for the lucky occupants of the upper floors.

In quick succession you now pass the sadly neglected, weather-boarded King's Head, The Angel (an angelic barmaid pulling a pint on its sign), and Tweedside Cottages, opposite which is St Mary's Convent. Carry on ahead, now on Putney Heath, and cross Dover House Road. Just after a bus stop but before a mini-roundabout, at a lodge house, turn left into Putney Park Lane.

The Angel, Roehampton

300-acre Putney Park never achieved the level of popularity as a royal hunting ground enjoyed by its near neighbour Richmond Park, leading to a dividing-up of the park into plots on which large mansions were built. One of these, Dover House, gave its name to the Dover House estate, built by the London County Council in 1921 on the former site of Putney Park.

Now your route lies arrow-straight along this gravel track, passing the old lodge house and gates of Dover House, the vast estate of well-built houses that replaced it, and two surviving Victorian buildings; Granard Lodge and St Margaret's church. Eventually as the track curves around The Pleasance, a green and tree-clad open space, look for a pathway on the right which you take to emerge in Woodborough Road. Turn left and carry on past a mixture of substantial older houses and more modern flats, then at Upper Richmond Road turn right, cross at the lights, and turn right for a few yards to the Northumberland Arms and Dyers Lane, where you turn left. At the end of this short cul-de-sac cross a railway footbridge and continue along Beauchamp Terrace, which swings round to the right to reveal Putney Common. Keep ahead past the fine houses on Lower Common South to meet Egliston Road at a sharp bend, by All Saints church.

Putney Lower Common is administered by the Wimbledon and Putney Commons Conservators, having been saved by an 1871 Act of Parliament from enclosure by the lord of the manor, Earl Spencer. The 40 acres of lightly-wooded common, home to sports pitches, the old buildings of Putney Hospital, and a rich diversity of wildlife, extend to Barnes Common and the lush greenery alongside Beverley Brook.

Putney Common

All Saints church, designed by GE Street and consecrated in 1874, has the distinction of possessing a large number of stained glass windows designed and manufactured by Edward Burne-Jones and Morris & Co in their beautiful 'Arts and Crafts' style, and is Grade II* listed.

Turn left to cut through the churchyard to the bus terminus and Lower Richmond Road at the Spencer Arms. Turn right and press on past an interesting variety of shops and cafés until you reach the Half Moon.

This is a real-ale pub with an enviable reputation for live music, where dozens of famous names have featured since folk and blues sessions started in the early 1960s. Still staging gigs seven days a week, the pub's Monday night acoustic sessions are a bargain at £2.50.

Turn right beside the pub to follow Biggs Row, cross Felsham Road and carry on along cottage-lined Charlwood Road, crossing Lacy Road on the way, to pass a barrier. Fork left, then turn sharp left along a paved way, Quill Lane, beside which stood The Quill, a friendly little pub that occupied this corner site just a few years ago. Keep ahead on Cardinal Place, passing several attractive side turnings, to meet Lacy Road again. There are two pubs here with outdoor seating, for a summertime drink; to the left, the Jolly Gardeners, and to the right, the Coat and Badge. Turn right to arrive at Putney High Street and the Exchange shopping centre (toilets on the first floor). Turn right (or left for buses to Wandsworth, Fulham etc. and Putney Bridge station for District line trains) and walk to the top of the High Street where you will find Putney station, and the end of your walk.

St Mary's church, Putney

SW14

12 Mortlake and East Sheen

Taking you far out into the leafy suburbs, this walk features a glimpse of historic Mortlake and the Thames riverside, before visiting Palewell Common and the willow-lined Beverley Brook, unobtrusively making its silent way through Richmond Park

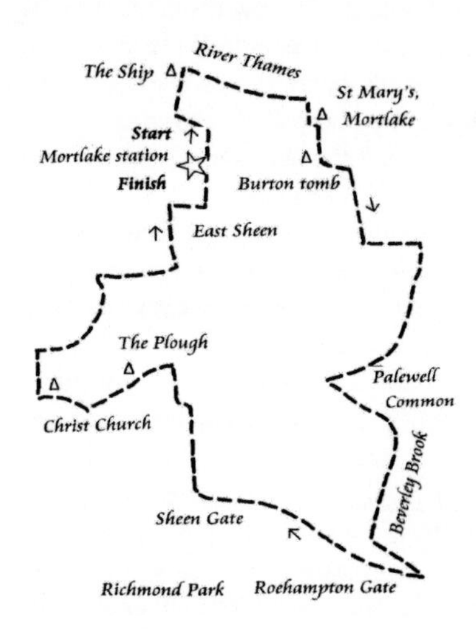

Distance	4½ miles.
Time	2-2½ hours.
Terrain	Pavements and footpaths, which can be muddy enough to require walking boots in wet weather.
Food and drink	A choice of cafés in East Sheen, a café at Roehampton Gate, and a snack kiosk at Palewell Common. There are several pubs on the route, including The Ship at Mortlake and The Plough at East Sheen.
Toilets	Sheen Lane, Mortlake, Palewell Common, Richmond Park.
Start and Finish	Mortlake station. Trains from Clapham Junction, Putney etc. Buses 33, 337, and 493 stop nearby in Upper Richmond Road, East Sheen, while Bus 419 calls at Ship Lane.

From Mortlake station turn left into Sheen Lane then straightaway bear left across Mortlake Green towards the industrial buildings and chimneys of the Stag brewery.

Beer has been brewed in Mortlake since the 15th century, at first for the monks of a religious foundation, and later, in the 18th century, as a commercial enterprise which grew apace as the owners acquired more land, even blocking off rights of way to the river to create Mortlake's major industry and local employer. London brewer Watney's eventually took over the business and for many years produced such iconic brands as Red Barrel, long forgotten now but as well-known two generations ago as the globally-promoted lager that the brewery now produces. In spite of these centuries of successful brewing current owners InBev recently announced the startling decision to close the whole operation by December 2010.

Cross at the lights by the Jolly Gardeners (what a likeable name for a pub) and walk down Ship Lane between the brewery buildings to reach the Thames at The Ship, which has toilets.

Reckoned to be Mortlake's oldest inn, The Ship would originally have served water-borne customers using the age-old landing stage, as well as locals who knew it at one time as the Harteshorne, later renamed the Blew Anchor. Since 1845 it has ably provided a fine vantage point to view the climax of the annual University Boat Race from Putney to Mortlake, the finishing point marked by an obelisk on the riverbank to your left, simply marked 'UBR'. Have a stroll along Thames Bank, where there are some fine old houses, notably Leyden House, Mortlake's oldest house, mainly 18th century but including some considerably older portions.

Turn right along the rough riverbank path, past the old brewery maltings, then at the first slipway you can either leave the riverbank, climb a flight of steps and turn left along Mortlake High Street to a zebra crossing, or if the river is not too high, carry on to the next steps at Tapestry Court and another access to the High Street. A plaque set into the ground here mentions the Lower Dutch House, part of the Mortlake Tapestry Works.

Tapestry of an amazing intricacy and beauty from these works still adorns the walls of many grand houses, stately homes, and palaces across the globe. Established in 1619, the company produced huge tapestries, using silk and wool enriched with silver and gold thread, woven by a workforce of specially-recruited Flemish weavers. Although the output was of the highest quality and much in demand, the business suffered from what we would today call cash-flow problems, with many of the long-suffering and unpaid weavers having to find other employment as the years went by and fashions changed. In 1703 the works finally closed, and today there are just one or two survivors of the original buildings.

St Mary's church

Go across the zebra crossing to enter the churchyard and walk past the front of St Mary's church.

St Mary's, whose tower dates from 1543 (don't believe the earlier inscription), replaced a 14th-century church that stood a little way to the west, near today's brewery site. The font, given by Archbishop Bourchier in 1486, is the only survivor from the old church. A ring of eight bells occupies the tower, six having been cast in 1694-95, and the last two in 1746. Not surprisingly the church has been much extended, altered, and restored during its long life, but still exhibits many interesting memorials within, some dating back to the 17th century. John Dee, scholar and astrologer to Queen Elizabeth I, is said to be buried in the chancel. In the churchyard, you may notice a finger-post pointing to Sir Richard Burton's tomb, an interesting relic further along your route.

Pass the churchyard and then turn left along an enclosed path beside a school. Turn first right to follow Worple Street, past a terrace of tiny cottages, then turn left at North Worple Way.

To view the Burton tomb, turn right here, then right at St Mary Magdalen church, where a door to the left gives access to the graveyard 9-3.30 Monday-Friday, 9-5 at weekends. The mausoleum, designed by Lady Burton in the form of a life-size tent, contains the gilt coffins of Sir Richard Burton (died 1890) explorer and translator of the Arabian Nights, and his wife Isobel.

Cross a footbridge over the railway lines, cross South Worple Way, then go straight ahead on Queen's Road, which once again is lined with a pleasing assortment of homely cottages. At Upper Richmond Road turn left and continue to a set of pedestrian lights where you cross and turn right to follow Hertford Avenue, a well-kept residential road which soon escapes the rush of the main road traffic. Pass Shene School and a run of allotments, then after a short and gentle incline turn left into Palewell Common.

Palewell Common originally extended to thirty acres, twelve of which became part of Richmond Park when it was walled-in as a hunting-ground for Charles I in 1637. Together with the adjacent Palewell Fields, it provides a very pleasant local green space, with a nine-hole putting green, tennis courts, sports fields, and woodland. The name suggests an area surrounded by a fence, or 'pale'.

Carry on past a snack kiosk, toilets, and playground to turn right alongside the Beverley Brook, which remains your companion as you leave the tarmac path to walk between fields and fence to a kissing gate by the perimeter wall of Richmond Park. Turn left through the gate and carry on beside the old brick wall all the way to Roehampton Gate. Go through the gate, pass the lodge (toilets and café to your left) and immediately turn right

The Beverley Brook flowing through Richmond Park

on the shared cycle track and path to cross over the brook again on a wooden bridge.

The 6½ mile long Beverley Brook rises in suburban south-west London and forms a delightful watery border to both Wimbledon Common and Richmond Park. It finally joins the Thames at Putney Embankment, and can easily be followed on a signed route, the Beverley Brook Walk. If time permits, stroll along the tree-shaded banks of the brook for a few minutes; you may be lucky enough to spot the iridescent blue flash of a kingfisher. The path that crosses the bridge here is part of the Tamsin Trail, a 7-mile circuit of the park, much used by cyclists, joggers, and of course walkers, who can complete a really varied and interesting circumnavigation of Richmond Park in 2½ to 3 hours, fortified by the sprinkling of cafés and pubs on or very near the route.

Press on uphill to a pond, where you can take either of the two paths, which join again at Sheen Gate. Turn right to leave the park here and walk straight ahead on Sheen Lane.

As you pass through the gate, glance back to spy, on the gatepost, a plaque in memory of a Richmond brewer named John Lewis who, in 1758, regained the public access that had been denied after Richmond Park had been closed by Sir Robert Walpole in the reign of George II. The ladderstiles and gates that had been in place since the park had been enclosed as a royal hunting-ground were reinstated, much to the delight of the locals.

Before a bend in the road cross at the refuge to continue on the left-hand side, with the Red House opposite. 150 yards on, turn left to follow Christ Church Road, passing The Plough, with Percy Lodge set back on the other side of the road.

There is some antiquity in this tranquil backwater of East Sheen; Percy Lodge, saved from demolition in 1926, was built around 1740, while the attractive group of cottages beside the road date from the 17th and 18th centuries. The Plough, a popular watering-hole with its rose-shaded tables and old-fashioned farm plough on show recently yielded fragments of a 15th-century wall during renovations.

Spencer Cottages

Keep on ahead as the road twists and turns to Christ Church, passing a pleasing medley of character cottages and houses, including Spencer Cottages.

Renowned architect Sir Arthur Blomfield designed Christ Church, his first church commission, which opened in 1863. Just before completion, poor construction caused the tower to collapse. It was duly rebuilt, and then in 1887 a north aisle was added.

Turn right beside the church along West Temple Sheen, passing Sheen Mount primary school and the Victoria pub. Turn right to follow Temple Sheen Road for ¼ mile to reach Upper Richmond Road, where you cross over by using the zebra crossing a few yards to the left, then turn right to pass Leinster Avenue and Elm Road, and a memory of bygone days at the little old house that still bears a sign proclaiming the variety of services offered by 'E Vine, chimney sweep, rubber dealer, work done with horse and van', and so on. Continue to Roebuck House and a supermarket car park, into which you turn and then follow the pavement to continue straight ahead between the lush gardens of Model Cottages. Turn right at St Leonard's Road, then left at Sheen Lane to the completion of your walk at Mortlake station.

Memories of past times, Upper Richmond Road

SW13, SW15

13 Barnes and Beverley Brook

A stroll around the historic village and riverside of Barnes, before embarking on a brisk stride across Barnes Common to the rowing Mecca of Putney Embankment

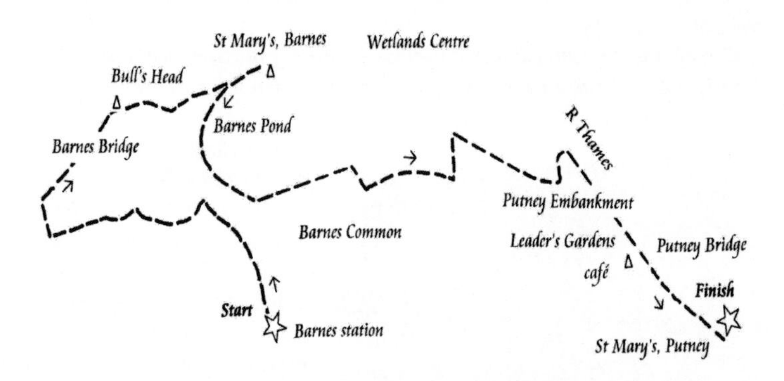

Distance	4 miles.
Time	2-2½ hours.
Terrain	Pavements, tarmac, and woodland paths which may be muddy in wet weather.
Food and drink	A choice of cafés and pubs in Barnes, Looloo's café on Putney Embankment, and at the end of the walk, St Mary's church café in Putney.
Toilets	Barnes Green, Putney.
Start	Barnes station. Trains to Richmond, Clapham Junction etc. Buses 33, 72, 265.
Finish	Putney Bridge. District line, Buses 14, 22, 39, 74, 85, 93, 220, 265, 270, 424, 430, 485. Putney rail station is within a few minutes' walk.

With your back to the original station building, which dates from 1846, go left to follow Station Road through a leafy bower of horse chestnut and one or two mature plane trees, all part of Barnes Common local nature reserve.

Barnes Common stretches to over 100 acres, including a large tract of dry acid grassland where many different grasses and wild flowers grow, the rarest of which is Burnet rose, unseen on any other common land in the London area. The land was much wetter years ago, so you may still see damp-loving plants such as lady's smock, purple moorgrass, and reeds. Heather used to be widespread but is now restricted to a few small patches. The high point of the common at Mill Hill is just 27ft above flood level, but proved to be a breezy spot when a hurricane in 1780 blew the wooden windmill completely over on to its side.

Carry on ahead at a mini-roundabout junction with Mill Hill Road, cross a bridge over Beverley Brook, and turn left to walk to the end of Willow Avenue.

Beverley Works

The impressive gateway of Beverley Works serves as a reminder of Omes Works, an enterprise that had started as a sawmill in 1904 and progressed to being a manufacturer of essential parts for vehicles and aircraft in World War II. In between times other products of the factory included starter motors and various car components, and even a car; the luxurious Beverley Barnes, fourteen of which were built. Barnes suffered a great deal during the Blitz, perhaps because the location of Omes had become known to the enemy.

At the end, branch off to the right to walk along Beverley Path, signed 'footpath to Barnes Bridge'. Cross Brookwood Avenue and ignore turnings to left and right to pass a row of cottages, soon after which the path dives under a low bridge to emerge at the end of Archway Street. Go ahead for 20 yards then fork right to follow Thorne Passage, passing more cosy cottages, to arrive at St Michael and All Angels church.

Say goodbye to Thorne Passage here and continue ahead on Charles Street to meet White Hart Lane. Turn right and cross with care to the left-hand side, then carry on to a roundabout junction with Mortlake High Street, where a café or two may tempt you to rest for a while. Cross at the zebra crossing and turn right towards the White Hart, a real-ale house where you can sip your drink by the water's edge. Just before the pub take the slipway down to the riverbank and turn right (or stay on the pavement if the tide is too high). Press on under the railway at Barnes Bridge station and continue along the concrete river wall.

Ye White Hart

Across the road, a couple of blue plaques on the handsome 18th-century villas lining The Terrace mention persons of note who have lived here, including Ninette De Valois, founder of the Royal Ballet, and a little further along, composer Gustav Holst. The instant appeal of a riverside residence, perhaps even with a veranda or balcony to enjoy the comings and goings on the water, explains why these old houses, in days gone by, were so popular as summer lets.

Soon you arrive at a roundabout by the Bull's Head.

Established in 1684, the Bull's Head still has the old stables, now a restaurant, for the horses of the many stagecoaches that passed through on their journey from Richmond to London. Completely rebuilt in 1845, it became a jazz venue in 1959, with sessions 7 nights a week and Sunday lunchtimes featuring top jazz names as well as new bands, with impromptu offerings from such greats as Charlie Watts, Jools Holland, and Sir Mick Jagger.

Turn right along Barnes High Street, passing the 18th-century Coach and Horses and one or two cafés, and then swing round to the left at Barnes pond to the popular Sun Inn. Press on ahead, now on Church Road, to negotiate a bend in the road and spy a row of shops and the well-patronised Petit Delice patisserie. Carry on ahead, crossing Kitson Road, all the way to St Mary's church.

A few yards ahead at the junction with Castlenau (but not on your route) is the entrance to the Wetlands centre, more than 100 acres of former reservoirs that opened as a bird reserve in 2000 through the vision and hard work of naturalist Sir Peter Scott. Well worth a visit at any time of the year, the variety of wildfowl, birds, and water-loving creatures of all kinds that can be seen (or heard) here is astonishing.

St Mary's has been expertly reconstructed after a devastating fire in 1978, started by vandals after the church had been left unlocked briefly. The oldest fabric of the church dates from the early 12th century, while the distinctive tower appeared c1485. The fire did produce one discovery; a blocked Norman doorway, unknown of before, was revealed in the former nave wall. Flanking the church are two early 18th-century houses, with the one on the left, Strawberry House, previously serving as the rectory.

St Mary's church, Barnes

After a moment spent in this peaceful haven, retrace your steps to the bend in the road, where you cross with care, using the nearby zebra crossing if necessary, and strike out across the Green, keeping to the left of the Barnes Green Centre. Keep ahead to skirt the pond, then turn left to the Old Sorting Office arts centre, which has a café, toilets, and outdoor tables by the Green. Keep on ahead through an avenue of horse chestnuts, which provide welcome shade if you are lucky enough to visit during the renowned Barnes Fair. Cross a little bridge over the Beverley Brook and fork left on a tarmac path, then before you come to a road bear left again, still on tarmac. Ignoring all side turnings, press on ahead across the green acres of Barnes Common to meet Rocks Lane. Cross at the pedestrian lights and branch to the right, signed 'Ranelagh Path'. Turn left beyond the fenced-in sports pitches to walk through a car park and continue between the high fence and the verdant dereliction of Barnes old cemetery, a sadly neglected place since having its railings removed in 1954, but still an important wildlife habitat. Maintain your direction as you undulate through woodland, with a sports field to your left. At the end of the field turn left on a rough grassy track to cross the Beverley Brook yet again, then turn right alongside the stream.

To your left are sports fields occupying the former site of the manor house, Barn Elms, the home of Sir Francis Walsingham, secretary of state to Queen Elizabeth I, from 1579 until his death in 1590. This grand medieval house, assessed for taxes in 1664 with a total of 23 hearths, was knocked down in 1694 and a new mansion built. In the 18th century the Hoare family of London bankers extended the house, which survived until demolition in 1954.

Beverley Brook

Keep on ahead through a lush world of fields, greenery, and birdsong for nearly ½ mile to meet the Thames at Putney Embankment. Turn right and cross the confluence of brook and river, and carry on all the way to Putney Bridge, pausing at Leader's Gardens, where you can spot the first exhibit on the Putney sculpture trail, and then visit Looloo's café, which is right by a playground and offers home-made food, a warm welcome, and customer toilet. Next on the route is an absorbing collection of rowing clubs and boat-houses, which have flourished here since the 1800s, then a little further along is the garden of the 18th-century Winchester House club, next door to the Duke's Head, a long-established Young's pub. Now you pass the huge Star and Garter hotel and mansions, built in Queen Victoria's day, then just before you leave the Embankment at Waterman's Green look out for an obelisk marked 'UBR'; the starting point of the annual University Boat Race to Mortlake.

Carry on ahead to Putney Bridge and St Mary's church (café here, and customer toilets), and the completion of your walk. A short stroll across the bridge brings you to Putney Bridge station, for District line trains, or turn right and walk to the top of the High Street for Putney rail station, and trains to Clapham Junction, Richmond etc. Bus stops nearby offer services to all local destinations.

Putney Embankment

SW11, SW18

14 Wandsworth Common

Playground, café, ponds, games, and cycling on the common; interesting old buildings, acres of open space, Northcote Road shops

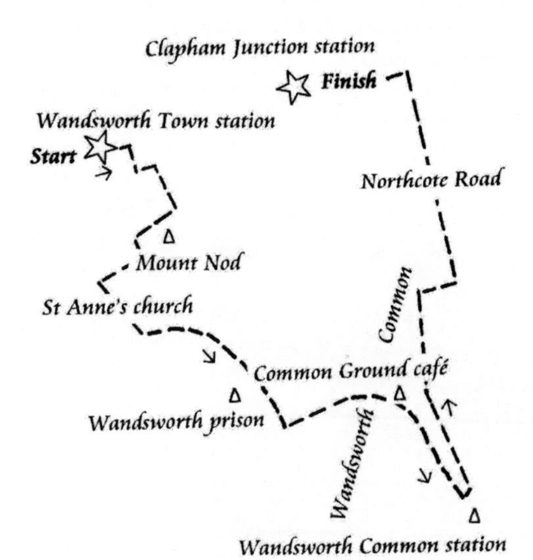

Distance	4¼ miles.
Time	2½ hours.
Terrain	Mostly level pavements with some minor slopes.
Food and drink	Old York Road, Wandsworth Common, Bellevue Terrace, Northcote Road.
Toilets	Wandsworth Common, Clapham Junction station.
Start	Wandsworth Town station. Trains to Clapham Junction, Putney, etc. Buses 28, 44.
Finish	Clapham Junction. Trains to all parts, Buses 35, 37, 39, 49, 77, 87, 156, 170, 219, 295, 337, G1, 319, 344, 345, C3.

From Wandsworth Town station cross Old York Road towards the green-tiled Alma pub, then turn left along Podmore Road.

The tempting attractions of Old York Road include the popular real-ale Alma, Brady's fish restaurant, two or three inviting cafés and several independent shops. This combination creates an appealing 'village', well away from the hurtling traffic on Wandsworth's hectic one-way system.

Pass the Royal Standard and then turn right to follow Dalby Road. Turn left along Dighton Road, continuing around a right-hand bend to follow Birdhurst Road on a tree-lined path. Cross East Hill at the lights and turn right, then after 40 yards, passing St Mary Magdalen Catholic church, turn left along a footpath through the Huguenot burial ground.

In the 17th and 18th centuries thousands of Huguenots (French Protestants) arrived in England, escaping religious persecution. Many settled in Wandsworth, bringing with them their skills in hat making, dyeing, and metal working, with the River Wandle as their source of power. This cemetery, known as Mount Nod, was the final resting place for many of them, their names inscribed on a plaque on the northern side of the plot.

Plaque at Mount Nod cemetery

Turn right at the end of the path to walk alongside railings to Book House, a handsome red-brick building of 1888. Cross with great care to the central island, then use the lights on the left to continue downhill on the left-hand pavement of East Hill. Turn left into Geraldine Road, where the United Reformed church sits on the corner. Take the first right turn, Eglantine Road, and continue to the end. Turn left into Aspley Road, then left again along St Ann's Crescent, passing St Anne's church (with the added 'e').

Built in 1822 by Robert Smirke, architect of the British Museum, St Anne's was one of the 'Waterloo churches' erected in celebration of England's victory over Napoleon. Badly damaged in WWII, and then losing its roof in a fire in 1950, the restored church with its 'pepper pot' tower stands as a distinctive local landmark.

St Anne's church

At the end of this road turn left to follow Allfarthing Lane, continuing straight on at a mini-roundabout. You are now on Heathfield Road, beside a fragment of Wandsworth Common. At a set of traffic lights continue straight ahead, after crossing to the right-hand pavement.

At this junction with Windmill Road you may wish to make a ¼ mile detour to see the windmill, minus its sails. If so, turn left, cross Trinity Road, and you will find it half-hidden amongst trees above the railway line. Of a type known as a smock mill, it was built in the 1830s to pump water from the newly-built London and South Western Railway cutting into the 'Black Sea', a lake situated nearby.

Carry on over the railway bridge and keep on ahead towards the grim outlines of Wandsworth Prison.

Originally opened as the Surrey House of Correction in 1851, Wandsworth is the largest prison in the London area and can house over 1600 prisoners. Famous past inmates include train robber Ronnie Biggs, East End gangster Reginald Kray, and in the 1890s playwright Oscar Wilde.

At the end of the prison buildings cross to the left-hand side of the road and then turn left along Alma Terrace, past a pleasing collection of rustic cottages, to the County Arms pub. Go across Trinity Road to Dorlcote Road, then after a very few yards leave the road and fork left down a gravel slope to a wide tree-lined tarmac path which you follow, accompanied by breezy acres of grass and sports fields to your left. Shortly you will come to a junction where you go half-right on a shared cycle track. To the left is the popular Common Ground café (and public toilets, behind the bowling green), making this an excellent refreshment stop.

Wandsworth Common's 175 acres were originally part of the manor of Battersea and Wandsworth, but passed to the Metropolitan Board of Works in 1887. A few years before this, the Rev John Craig chose this spot to build an enormous telescope, apparently powerful enough to enable letters ¼ of an inch high to be read from half a mile away. It lasted less than twenty years, a victim of poor visibility due to pollution.

The Common Ground café

At the next junction do not cross the railway bridge, but instead bear right alongside the railway fence, passing a succession of reed-fringed ponds. Give yourself a moment to trace the paths around this watery corner of the common, the perfect place for a picnic. This path ends at Bellevue Road, with Wandsworth Common station opposite. There are one or two pubs and cafés here. Turn left over the railway bridge, then straightaway go left again to walk alongside the other side of the railway tracks. Eventually you will come to the footbridge that you met earlier; at this point fork right on a shared cycle path to Bolingbroke Grove, which you follow left to arrive at the Stock Pond. Cross at the refuge and continue on the right-hand pavement, then take the first right, Bramfield Road. Now you drop down to the shops and cafés of Northcote Road, where a left turn will lead you into the heart of this fascinating street.

Popular café Crumpet, with children's play area, cakes, and organic food from local suppliers is one of Northcote Road's many attractions, which also include Dove butchers, here since the 1880s, the well-stocked Bolingbroke Bookshop, and market stalls offering everything from crafts to cabbages. Originally clustered around the newly-built Clapham Junction station in the 1860s, all the stalls moved here in 1910 when St John's Road was developed. When you come to Battersea Rise glance to the right to see two interesting old buildings: the Thomas Memorial church of the Nazarene, and the former Temperance billiard hall, with tiled fascia and tower, now a pub.

At the traffic lights at Battersea Rise keep ahead along St John's Road, past all the well-known high street shops, to Lavender Hill and the unmistakeable grandeur of Debenhams store, formerly Arding & Hobbs. Cross over and turn left for a few yards on St John's Hill to the end of your walk at 'Britain's busiest railway station', Clapham Junction, or catch one of the numerous buses from here, serving a wide choice of destinations.

SWII

15 Battersea

A boating lake, children's zoo, and masses of space for games in Battersea Park, plus a tour of old Battersea 'village' and riverside

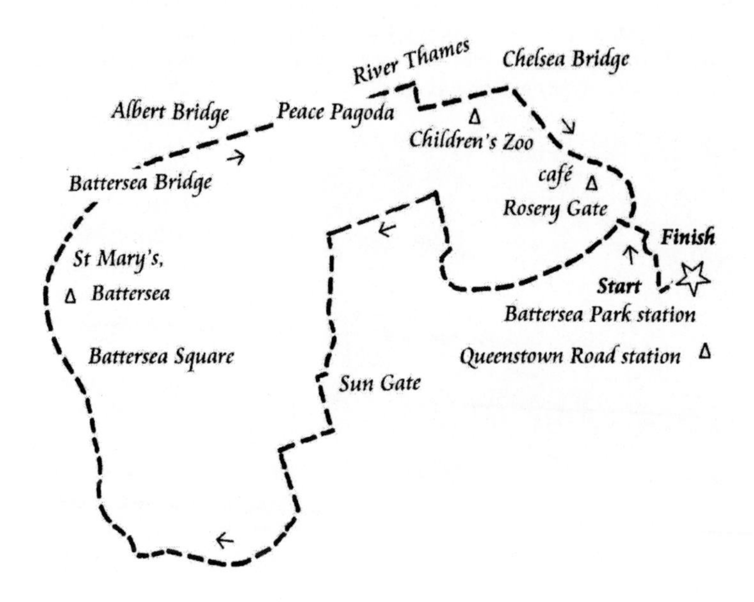

Distance	5½ miles.
Time	3 hours.
Terrain	Gravel and tarmac paths, pavements, and cobbled streets.
Food and drink	Battersea Park and Square.
Toilets	Battersea Park.
Start and Finish	Battersea Park station. Trains from Victoria, Clapham Junction etc. Buses 44, 137, 156, 344, 452. Queenstown Road station, for trains to Waterloo, Putney etc. is close by.

Turn right from Battersea Park station on Battersea Park Road (note the fine iron bridge and London, Brighton and South Coast Railway crest, 1865, overhead). Cross ahead at the lights then turn right along Queenstown Road to Queen's Circus, where you have a fine view of the Nine Elms gasholders, and a peep at the chimneys of Battersea Power Station. Once across Prince of Wales Drive turn into Battersea Park through Rosery Gate. Go straight ahead across the carriage drive to walk past the rose beds of the first portion of Rosery Gardens, then turn left at the first crossing path to stroll beside the lake.

Away to your left are the grand mansions lining Prince of Wales Drive, while across the lake herons flap lazily to and from their island treetop nests. On your way, you will see a bold piece of sculpture by Barbara Hepworth; 'Single Form', dating from 1961-62. The lake, dug in 1860, has to be one of the most beautiful of any in a London park.

'Single Form' in Battersea Park

At a T-junction turn right, then fork left through the sub-tropical gardens.

An information board here explains the work carried out by John Gibson, Park superintendent for 14 years from 1856, who with James Pennethorne was the driving force in the design and construction of Battersea Park. This area had always been known as Battersea Fields, a wasteland of low-lying marshes, with a scattering of somewhat disreputable inns and minor pleasure gardens, which were a magnet for undesirables. Even an occasional duel took place, the best known being between the Duke of Wellington and Lord Winchilsea in 1829; the Duke deliberately missed, whereupon his opponent fired into the air, and honour was restored. The idea of a public park first came from influential London builder Thomas Cubitt in 1844, after which the protracted processes of land purchase commenced. Soil was brought in vast quantities from the excavations for London's docks to raise the land level, while the lowest and wettest part was earmarked for the lake. 40,000 trees and even more bushes were planted, bestowing the wooded beauty that the park enjoys today. Palms, tree-ferns, and bananas were grown in the sub-tropical garden, and an alpine garden created a backdrop for the lake. Queen Victoria performed the opening ceremony in 1858, and the park soon became tremendously popular, especially after cyclists were allowed to use the carriage drives for the first time in any London park. In more recent times the park hosted the Festival of Britain in 1951, and still has a few surviving reminders of the event.

Ignore the first left turn, then take the second left (to see another piece of sculpture, 'Three Standing Figures' by Henry Moore, keep on ahead and then left for a few yards) and carry on (or turn right for the Pump House art gallery and information centre) past a bowling green to the bandstand. There are fountains, a tea terrace, and toilets, straight ahead. At the bandstand turn left along Central Avenue to meet the carriage drive, where you turn left, passing a playground on your left. Soon you come to a wide junction, where you bear right and say goodbye to the park for now as you leave through Sun Gate. Go left to cross Prince of Wales Drive, then go to the right across Albert Bridge Road, into which you then turn. Take the first on the right, Kersley Street, and turn left at the end, with St Stephen's church occupying the corner. Cross straight over Battersea Park Road to follow Latchmere Road. At Latchmere leisure centre go across the pedestrian crossing, then twist left and immediately right along a cobbled lane which leads under a succession of three railway bridges and two welcome green spaces, Falcon Park and Shillington Gardens.

Memories of the 1951 Festival of Britain in Battersea Park

Keep on ahead, now on Cabul Road, past one or two interesting old converted buildings. Cross Candahar Road and pass Christ Church, with its peaceful garden alongside. Turn left for a few yards on meeting Battersea Park Road again, where The Asparagus pub recalls the days when this locality was famed for its market garden produce, notably lavender and 'Battersea Bundles' of asparagus. Cross right at the lights, then go straight ahead on Battersea High Street, past a short parade of shops, a café, and pub, and perhaps a few stalls. Press on past a barrier and under a bridge.

As you wend your way along the High Street, there is much of interest; two traditional pubs, the Castle and The Woodman, and to the right, Sacred Heart church, opened in 1893, with its mighty spire. Next along is Le Quecum wine bar, which features Gypsy Swing music for entertainment, while Thomas's, originally Sir Walter St John's school brings you back to earth with the sombre motto 'Rather Deathe than False of Faythe'. The school was established in 1700, with the present buildings dating from 1859. To lighten the mood, the pavement cafés of Battersea Square soon appear, with welcome benches nearby. There are still a few echoes of the old riverside village of Battersea here; the Dutch-gabled 17th-century former pub, The Raven, now a bar and deli, 'Bennett, London House, established 1780' emblazoned on a wall, and Ship House, an old warehouse.

Battersea Square

Cross to the left at the traffic lights and then continue ahead on Battersea Church Road to St Mary's church, overshadowed in size but not in style by the wedge-shaped Montevetro apartments, completed in 2001.

Sitting proudly by the old slipway down to the Thames foreshore, St Mary's has been the nucleus of the original riverside settlement of Battersea since the first Saxon church of about 800 AD. The elegant church that you see today dates from 1777, and contains several interesting 17th and 18th-century monuments.

Go through a fine pair of wrought-iron gates to pass the front of the church, and then press on beside the river all the way to Battersea Bridge, which opened in 1890 to designs by famous engineer Sir Joseph Bazalgette. It replaced a narrow wooden structure that had been in service since 1771.

Encompassed in your view from here are Chelsea Harbour, with its Belvedere tower topped with a sliding ball that moves with the tide, the shell of Lots Road power station, now generating no more and awaiting grand development plans, the rust-red geometric shapes of the World's End estate, and houseboat-lined Cheyne Walk.

Cross Battersea Bridge Road with great care at the refuge and then carry on beside the river past the curvaceous Albion flats, where the most is made of the Thames view, and then past Foster and Partners architects offices (note the miniature Gherkin in the window). A little bridge guides you over an ancient dock entrance, still fitted with lock gates. Finally you arrive at Albert Bridge Road, which you cross with care to go through a pedestrian gate into Battersea Park once more.

Fortune has spared the graceful outlines of Albert Bridge for us to enjoy today; it had been scheduled for replacement fifty years ago, but was saved at the last minute, and is now supported by a central prop. The bridge first opened in 1873, and is an unusual cantilever and suspension combination, and still sports the original toll booths, with marching instructions for troops crossing over.

Follow the riverside all the way to the Buddhist Peace Pagoda, which has occupied this spot since 1985. Turn right to the roadway, where a left turn soon brings you to the Children's Zoo.

A fascinating selection of animals live here, including meerkats, monkeys and lemurs, owls and a mynah bird, pigs, chickens, and so on. Stick insects, mice and huge snails cannot fail to appeal to all youngsters, who can also have a great time in the play area. There is a café, and plenty of room for picnics, and the zoo is open daily from 10 a.m.

St Mary's church, Battersea

Continue past the zoo and a toilet block to arrive at a roundabout. Turn right to pass a barrier, then carry on past tennis courts, the Thrive garden project, Millennium arena, and a little further along an exercise area, boating lake (boats for hire) and La Gondola waterside café. This might be a good time to stop for refuelling, as your walk is nearly finished. Carry on past the café, through a bower of more of the park's wonderful old trees, and then turn left to leave through Rosery Gate. Turn right to cross Prince of Wales Drive and retrace your steps along Queenstown Road to Battersea Park station, where the walk ends.

Battersea Park station (below) and Albert Bridge (above)

John Innes Park (Walk 25)

Above: Beverley Brook (Walk 12). Below: St John's church, Fulham (Walk 9)

Above: Norwood Grove (Walk 23). Below: Wandsworth Common (Walk 14)

Putney Embankment (Walk 13)

Rassell's, Earl's Court (Walk7)

Above: King George's Park (Walk 20). Below: Tooting Common (Walk 19)

Above: Queen Victoria and Kensington Palace (Walk 4). Below: Rushmere Pond (Walk29)

Above: Wandle meets Thames (Walk 10). Below: Stockwell Artists' Studios (Walk16)

SW8, SW9

16 Stockwell

Grand old houses, a go-karting track, an adventure playground, and a house where Vincent Van Gogh once lived; this walk is full of surprises, and even includes a pub called The Surprise

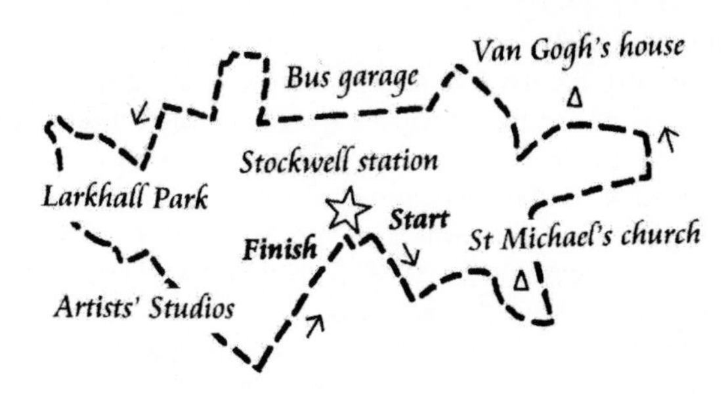

Distance	3 miles.
Time	1½-2 hours.
Terrain	Level pavements throughout.
Food and drink	A limited selection of cafés and pubs in Stockwell and Wandsworth Road, including the Priory Arms in Lansdowne Way and The Surprise at Larkhall Park.
Toilets	No public toilets on the route, however the refuelling stops mentioned above mostly provide customer toilets.
Start and Finish	Stockwell station. Northern and Victoria lines, Buses 2, 88, 155, 196, 333, 345, P5.

Walk straight ahead out of Stockwell station and cross Clapham Road. Turn left to then cross Stockwell Road, into which you turn. Take the first left, St Michael's Road, which is lined with respectably solid 19th-century houses. At the end of this road turn right into Stockwell Park Crescent, passing more houses of quality.

Although the major housing developments hereabouts occurred in the mid-1800s, the manor of Stockwell dates from the late 13th century. A manor house once stood near Stockwell Green, another village green obliterated by bricks and mortar, leaving the church of St Andrew, which is a little way off your route, as a lone memory of the old village centre. Built in 1767, it is Lambeth's second-oldest church, its age concealed beneath a mundane exterior.

Turn left to follow Stockwell Park Road, where you will pass Slade Gardens adventure playground and St Michael's parish church, which dates from 1841. After passing the church, at a kink in the road, turn right to continue to the end of Groveway.

Beneath your feet here is the old course of the River Effra, one of London's lost rivers, which flowed through Brixton to the Thames at Vauxhall. Restricted now to an underground pipe, in times of heavy downpours it comes to life again, and can be seen issuing from a storm relief channel next to Vauxhall Bridge.

At Brixton Road turn left to walk past several 18th-century houses, amazing survivors of bombs, developers, and town planners, until you arrive at a set of pedestrian lights, where you go left to follow Hillyard Street.

When you come to the junction with Hackford Road, before you cross over and continue ahead, turn right for 20 yards to number 87, which sports a blue plaque in honour of Vincent Van Gogh, who lived here from 1873-74 while working for art dealer Goupil & Co.

Carry on ahead to follow Durand Gardens, passing Liberty Street. Continue round a right-hand bend and past a railed-off oval of woodland to meet Clapham Road. Turn left and walk to a set of traffic lights, passing some imposing Georgian mansions. Cross to the right to follow Lansdowne Way past one or two cafés and small shops. If you wish to break your journey at

Stockwell bus garage

this half-way point simply continue on Clapham Road for the short distance to Stockwell station, otherwise press on along Lansdowne Way, crossing South Lambeth Road (with the cream-painted portico of Stockwell Baptist church to your right) until you arrive at Stockwell bus garage.

Built between 1951-54, this concrete cathedral of transport has a 400ft long parking area arched over with roof spans 194ft long, reaching a height of 54ft. the total area of 73,000 sq ft can accommodate over 200 buses. Vast and utilitarian, it has achieved English Heritage Grade II* listing.

Once past the bus garage turn right to follow Guildford Road. Take the first left, opposite a mellow old church building, into St Barnabas Villas, then turn left and left again along Lansdowne Gardens, which sports a small central green amongst the proud old villas. On meeting Lansdowne Way again turn right, cross at a zebra crossing and keep on ahead to turn left at Priory Grove, by the Priory Arms, a popular 'local' serving food and real ale. Carry on past a go-kart track and a (locked) activity centre, then turn right into Priory Mews, through an arbour and seating space, to enter Larkhall Park.

One of Stockwell's most popular pubs

Until it closed a few years ago there used to be a local hostelry called the Larkhall Tavern. It had been named after a nearby mansion, Lark Hall, and now the name is kept alive in this welcome green space. The park saw completion in the 1970s from plans drawn up 30 years earlier, to provide more open space amongst dense housing, after extensive bomb damage in the Blitz.

Keep right to pass a playground, then turn left to The Surprise, another pub with homely attractions that are hard to resist. Walk the few yards to Wandsworth Road where you turn left. Another inn and one or two cafés are among the parade of useful shops here. After a few yards branch left across a wide paved space to re-enter Larkhall Park. Follow the tarmac path on the right of the information board, passing another playground, and then a fenced-off sports pitch, where you fork left to leave the park at Larkhall Lane. Turn left, then take the first right, Jeffreys Road. Press on past the Methodist church, opposite which is an ivy-covered, curiously fascinating old relic of a building, which turns out to be the home of Stockwell Artists' Studios, once a hospital with a long and fulsome history.

Clapham Maternity Hospital was the first hospital to have an all-female staff, with female medical students trained only by women. Founded in 1889 by Dr Annie McCall and Marion Ritchie, the hospital at first took in poor women and unmarried mothers, and later went on to become a much-loved local institution. Over the years many thousands of parents were to be grateful for the care they and their little ones received here, and for the unique tranquillity of the specially-designed gardens. This success required a new building, the one you see today (designed by a woman), in a classical style of 1915. In 1935 the name changed to the Annie McCall Maternity Hospital, then after severe bomb damage in 1940 and amalgamation into the NHS, the hospital closed in the 1970s. Of the many local people who were born here, probably the best-known is actor Roger Moore, on October 14th 1927.

At the end of Jeffreys Road turn left to walk along Clapham Road for 350 yards to the end of this round trip, and your Tube or bus home from Stockwell station.

Old and new dwellings, Clapham Road

SW4, SW9

17 Clapham Park and Brixton

Fashionable villas, a hidden windmill, and Brixton's amazing markets

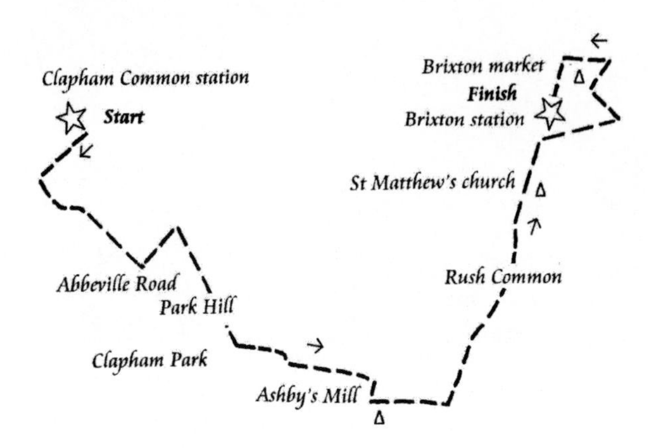

Distance	2½ miles.
Time	1½ hours.
Terrain	Pavement and tarmac with some gentle slopes.
Food and drink	Clapham's High Street and Old Town should cater for most tastes, while Brixton's market streets offer an exotic choice.
Toilets	Brixton.
Start	Clapham Common station. Northern line, Buses 35, 37, 50, 88, 137, 155, 322, 345, 417.
Finish	Brixton station. Victoria line, Overground trains to Bromley South, Victoria etc. Buses 2, 3, 35, 37, 45, 59, 109, 118, 133, 159, 196, 250, 333, 355, 415, 432, P4, P5.

From the clock tower at Clapham Common station, with your back to the glass-domed station roof, cross right at the lights to turn right along Clapham Common South Side. Continue past the Alexandra pub, the parade of shops, and mansion-lined Crescent Grove, 60 yards after which you turn left to walk along Crescent Lane. Following the lane's twists and turns, you will pass St Mary's school, and arrive at Abbeville Road, a popular setting for a range of independent shops and cafés, a little further along the street to the right. To continue your walk however, turn left, cross the road, and take the second on the right, Park Hill.

19th-century villas in Park Hill

Prolific London builder Thomas Cubitt, creator of the fine stucco terraces of Pimlico and Belgravia, commenced the development of Clapham Park from around 1830 onwards, building villas for the well-to-do on wide thoroughfares such as King's Avenue. As you stroll along Park Hill you will see several of the original villas, which date from 1830-50. In later years the attractive terraces centred on Abbeville Road were built, many of them on the former grounds of some of the Georgian mansions on Clapham Common South Side. Lincoln House, Thomas Cubitt's own 14-bedroom mansion, must have surpassed all the other houses on the estate with luxuries such as an aviary, extensive gardens containing flowers, fruit, and tree-shaded walks, and a stable yard for four carriages and horses. The house survived until 1905.

Continue along Park Hill until you once again meet Crescent Lane, into which you turn left. Go straight across King's Avenue to a T-junction with Lyham Road. Turn right and almost immediately left past a barrier, on a paved and concrete path beside a line of mostly empty shops. Pass another barrier and press on ahead, maintaining the same direction, through Ramillies Close, between modern low-rise housing with a shrubbery alongside. At the end of the planted area you will arrive at an open space where you turn right to follow a path towards Windmill Gardens and Ashby's Mill.

Ashby's Mill

The mill was built for John Ashby around 1816, and ground corn for the local farmers until encroaching buildings reduced the force of the wind, the problem being solved by conversion to steam and then gas power. According to a local guidebook, Ashby's Mill was still grinding corn in 1924, but ceased working ten years later. Look out for an old millstone lying in the grass nearby, and a glimpse of Brixton Prison further uphill, the original buildings of which date from 1820, just after the mill appeared on this hillside.

From Windmill Gardens keep on past another barrier and continue, now on Blenheim Gardens, to Brixton Hill, which you cross at the lights and then turn left to carry on downhill. Once across Brixton Water Lane take the path half-right across Rush Common, opposite the imposing edifice of Corpus Christi Catholic church. Follow this tarmac path the full length of the common to rejoin Brixton Hill, where you continue your downhill route across the busy junction with St Matthew's Road, and past St Matthew's church.

Rush Common is a wide strip of land alongside Brixton Hill, much of which was appropriated by Victorian house-builders to add the attraction of a long front garden, still evident at some of the older properties further up the hill. Lambeth Council is slowly restoring the common as a long-term project.

St Matthew's, here since 1824, started life as one of the 'Waterloo Churches' built to celebrate victory over France. It is Brixton's oldest church, with room for a congregation of 2,000, and in recent times has adapted to being not only a church but also a community venue. Faintly discernible on one of the gateposts is the instruction for 'Carriages to enter at this gate'. Across the busy main road, displaying a tasteful Edwardian blend of brick and stone is the impressive Lambeth Town Hall, dating from 1908.

From the central island just past the Budd family memorial cross right and walk across Brixton Oval to the Tate library, then turn left to the Ritzy cinema.

The bust of Sir Henry Tate, a resident of Streatham, in front of the library that he endowed recalls the man who benefited the nation by bringing us not only the Tate Gallery, but also the humble sugar cube. The inscription tells us that he was an 'upright merchant' and a 'wise philanthropist'.

Turn right at the cinema to follow Coldharbour Lane. Cross Electric Lane and Rushcroft Road, then at the traffic lights just before the railway bridge turn left along Atlantic Road. Market Row on the left and Brixton Village to the right are two well-patronized examples of the town's distinctive covered markets.

Electric Avenue

Now your walk comes to a lively conclusion as you take a short tour through Brixton's market streets, with the opportunity to explore a labyrinth of indoor and outdoor stalls, selling just about everything under the sun. The original 'village' of Brixton, the name derived from 'Brixe's Stone', an ancient boundary marker of the manor of Lambeth, had its origins on Brixton Hill. A move downhill came once the railway opened up the area in the 1860s, when Brixton became a thriving town, with shops such as Bon Marche, one of the first ever department stores and eventually part of the John Lewis group, opening in 1877. In the 1880s Electric Avenue became one of the first streets to be lit by electricity, followed in 1911 by the opening of the Electric Pavilion, now the Ritzy cinema, London's oldest cinema still used for its original purpose. For many years the town centre maintained its position as one of south London's major shopping attractions, and although today the grandeur may have diminished somewhat, Brixton still has bags of verve and character.

Just before a high railway viaduct crosses diagonally overhead, turn right along Popes Road, where there are public toilets. Go under a bridge and turn left along Brixton Station Road, with the Recreation Centre on your right. Carry on to the end of this road of market stalls, then turn left on Brixton Road. The walk ends at this busy spot, where you can turn left along Atlantic Road for 120 yards to catch an Overground train to Victoria, Herne Hill etc. or carry on straight ahead for 100 yards to Brixton Underground station, and buses to all parts.

SW4, SW11

18 Clapham

Many buildings of interest, a multitude of places for young ones to play, and a chance to explore Clapham Common's attractions, followed by tea or a picnic by the bandstand

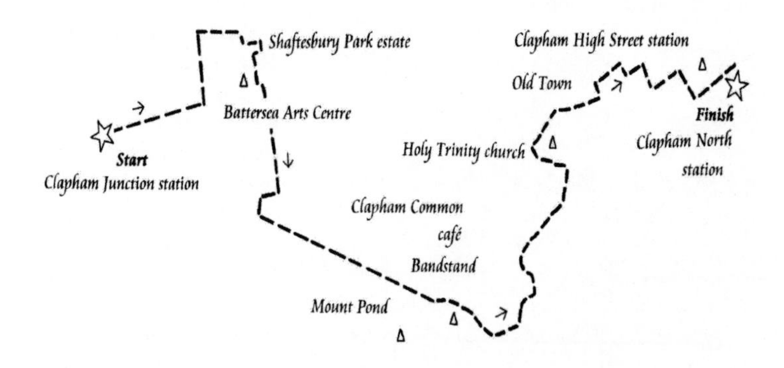

Distance	4 miles.
Time	2 hours.
Terrain	Tarmac paths, pavements, grass, 3 gentle hills.
Food and drink	Clapham Junction, Common, Old Town, and High Street.
Toilets	Clapham Junction station, Windmill Road.
Start	Clapham Junction station. Trains from all parts, Buses 35, 37, 39, 49, 77, 87, 156, 170, 219, 295, 319, 337, 344, 345, C3, G1.
Finish	Clapham North station. Northern line, Buses 50, 88, 155, 322, 345, P5.

Leave Clapham Junction station by the exit for Town Centre, and turn left to cross Falcon Road, opposite the famous Arding & Hobbs store, now Debenhams.

There are several buildings of note here; a few yards behind you, up St John's Hill, stands the Clapham Grand, built in 1900 as a theatre and variously used as a music hall, cinema, and Bingo hall, and now a live music venue and nightclub. The sumptuous interior boasts the largest flashing dance floor in Europe. Across the road the former Arding & Hobbs store is one of South London's best-known landmarks. Built in 1885, the flamboyant cupola was added after a fire in 1909. Back on your side of the road, the Falcon inn once featured on a popular engraving of 1801, at a time when the inn had a landlord by the name of Robert Death. Artist John Nixon happened to see a group of undertakers refreshing themselves here, and published a print of 'Undertakers at Death's Door'.

The Falcon, Clapham Junction

Carry on ahead to climb Lavender Hill, passing Falcon Lane and a superstore, then turn left along Dorothy Road. Now you come across Lavender Gardens, which has a small playground. At the foot of a short hill turn right to follow Amies Street, passing what used to be Lavender Hill school, one of many substantial and impressive schools built at the end of the 19th century. At Latchmere Road turn right, cross at the lights, then turn left downhill. Cross Heathwall Street then take the next right at Sabine Road, opposite the Fox and Hounds pub.

Now you enter the Shaftesbury Park estate, recalling social reformer Lord Shaftesbury, who held the post of president of the Artisans, Labourers and General Dwelling Company at the time this estate was laid out on former market gardens. Designed to improve the living conditions of the working classes, these neat, tree-shaded cottages were erected 1873-77, with the crest of the Artisans Company proudly displayed above many of the porches.

Take the first right turn into Elsley Road, which swings left, and then turn right into Eland Road. Take the first right again into Heathwall Street, cross to the left-hand side and then turn left between bollards to climb Town Hall Road. Continue past the Grand Hall entrance of the former Town Hall, which now houses Battersea Arts Centre, to arrive at the front of the building, passing two classic red telephone boxes on the way.

Local architect EW Mountford designed what was then called Battersea Town Hall, which opened its doors in 1893. Over the years dances, shows, talent contests, and jazz performances were staged in the Grand and Lower Halls, the latter becoming an air raid shelter in the last war. In 1965 Battersea became part of Wandsworth borough, and since then the building has narrowly escaped demolition after a vociferous local campaign, to become a thriving arts enterprise once again.

Cottages in Eland Road

Go across Lavender Hill at the pedestrian lights and turn left.

Take the first right to stroll along Sisters Avenue, alongside some stylish Victorian houses. As this road goes left, carry on ahead along Marjorie Grove to arrive at Clapham Common North Side. Turn right for 75 yards and cross at the lights to go straight ahead onto the common on a tarmac path, then turn left before a children's playground. Press on along this wide path among a variety of mature trees to a road junction with The Avenue, where you use two zebra crossings to maintain your straight-line direction, with woodland to your right and acres of open space to the left.

Dramatically thrusting upwards above the treetops to your left are the bold outlines of Cedars Terraces, part of a varied medley of grand houses, villas, and mansions that encircle the common. They are all described in an excellent guidebook by the Clapham Society, available at Clapham Books, in the High Street.

Keep going all the way to the Bandstand, which offers a fine picnic spot with plenty of benches, or a chance for a break at the café here.

Splendidly restored in 2006, the bandstand is London's largest and oldest, dating from 1890. The design is a copy of an original that once adorned the gardens of the Royal Horticultural Society in South Kensington. Away to your right is Mount Pond, one of four ponds on the common. The 'mount' in the middle of the pond was an 18th-century whim of wealthy local resident Henton Brown, who liked the pond so much he kept his own boat moored here.

Go left of the bandstand to take the second path to the right of the café, heading towards another playground. Behind the playground (where you will find public toilets) turn right then left along Windmill Drive to the Windmill on the Common pub. Turn left past the front of the pub and carry on until you meet the main road, then go left on a tarmac path towards Long Pond. Skirt round the left-hand side of the pond to turn right on a path with netball courts to your left.

Sports of all kinds have been played on the common for centuries; archery, football, golf, and horse riding were always popular, and the Greater London Horse Show drew the crowds for thirty years, continuing until 1985. More recently the common has been subjected to several mammoth events and concerts which have not been universally applauded, especially with the locals, not to mention the resident wildlife.

Cross Rookery Road and carry on ahead to go across Long Road with care at the refuge, then maintaining your direction keep on to the statue-topped drinking fountain. Take the second path on the left, with a vast paddling pool away to your right, to arrive in front of Holy Trinity church.

Holy Trinity church

An Act of Parliament paved the way for this church to be built on common land, after a decision had been made to replace St Paul's, the ancient parish church in Rectory Grove, where the old village and manor house once stood. Holy Trinity was built 1774-76 and contained box pews, galleries, and a lofty three-tier pulpit. Beneath the belfry is the original clock, made by Thwaites of Clerkenwell.

Walk past the church to the road and turn right on Clapham Common North Side. Cross The Pavement at the zebra crossing and then carry on ahead towards the bus depot, where you fork right at The Polygon (not sharp right) passing the Rose and Crown pub. Another pedestrian crossing guides you across Old Town and straight on into Grafton Square, which boasts a playground, gardens, and a handsome array of decorous mid-Victorian terraced houses.

Old Town, Clapham

Old Town certainly lives up to its name. To your left as you passed The Polygon are several elegant, well-proportioned houses of the 18th century, one of which, Sycamore House of 1787, housed a very busy laundry. Even the days of Queen Anne are remembered here, in a row of immaculate 300-year-old dwellings, beyond which Rectory Grove winds round to the old parish church of St Paul's. These antique pleasures are not on your route, but are well worth the short diversion of only a few minutes.

Turn left at the far side of the square, then right into Belmont Road, and then right again into Belmont Close (note the Odd Fellows Hall of 1852), where you continue past a barrier into Stonhouse Street. After 15 yards turn left under an arch and go ahead on a paved area, then a short access road, to turn right opposite a terrace of old cottages on Clapham Manor Street. This is one of Clapham's oldest streets, evident in the diverse mixture of architectural styles here. Take the first left into Voltaire Road, then at a crossroads turn right into Edgeley Road, where you can spot winged dragons displayed on Pearson Mews. Turn left at Clapham High Street.

Facing you are some interesting old buildings, including the arch-roofed former Temperance Billiard Hall, with domed and tiled entrance, the best example of several such halls built in London to encourage the working man away from the temptations of the pub. This splendidly-restored local landmark dates from 1908-10.

Carry on along the High Street until just before a railway bridge you have a choice, as the walk ends here; either turn left for Clapham High Street railway station, or cross at the pedestrian lights and continue under the bridge for 150 yards to Clapham North station, on the Northern line.

The Drinking Fountain on Clapham Common

SW12, SW16, SW17

19 Balham and Tooting Bec

Explore some interesting backwaters of the 'Gateway to the South', have a good run about on the common, and maybe a dip at the Lido

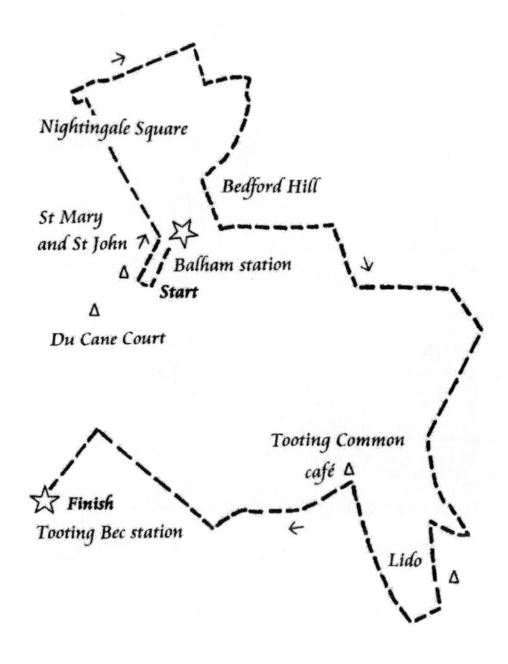

Distance	4¾ miles.
Time	2½ hours.
Terrain	Pavements and tarmac, with some uneven gravel paths.
Food and drink	Plenty of pubs and cafés in Balham, and the café on the common.
Toilets	Balham, Tooting Common.
Start	Balham station. Northern line, buses 155, 249, 355.
Finish	Tooting Bec station. Northern line, buses 155, 219, 249, 319, 355.

Take the station exit for High Road (east) and turn left under the railway bridge (toilet here). After 150 yards go over the pedestrian crossing and turn right, back towards the bridge.

As you crossed the road, to your left is Du Cane Court, an Art Deco block consisting of over 670 apartments, built 1935-38. At that time it was said to be the largest block of privately owned flats under one roof in Europe. Local legend attests that Adolf Hitler had earmarked the building for his HQ, which could explain why it survived WWII intact. When you turn right the Grade II listed church of St Mary and St John the Divine presents its handsome exterior, enhanced by an unusual domed baptistery and a clock tower reminiscent of one of Wren's City churches. Opened as a chapel in 1808, and enlarged in stages over nearly a century, the church as you see it today saw completion by 1903.

St Mary and St John the Divine

Go past the church and continue back under the bridge. Turn immediately left to follow Chestnut Grove, and continue for ¼ mile, ignoring all side turnings, to arrive at Nightingale Square. Turn left, then right, along the other side of the square, passing the Church of the Holy Ghost and Oak Lodge School. At the far end cross Endlesham Road and go straight ahead on Temperley Road. This quiet residential road ends at a T-junction, where you turn right along cottage-lined Bellamy Street, then turn left, with The Grove pub on the corner, to follow Oldridge Road as far as Balham High Road. Turn right and use the pedestrian crossing to continue on the left-hand pavement back towards the centre of Balham, passing the Devonshire pub on the way.

By the late 1800s many of the small estates and farms hereabouts had been engulfed by new housing developments, and not long after this Bedford Hill and the High Road became a noted shopping centre, complete with a department store. In 1903 the horse tramway from Westminster to Tooting celebrated electrification with a visit from the future King George V, who not only paid his fare but travelled through Balham on a flower-bedecked tram to the terminus at Totterdown Street.

After ¼ mile, opposite a supermarket and Balham library (toilets here) turn left to follow Bedford Hill. Hildreth Street, on the right, has a café or two and a small market. Take the third turning on the left, Sistova Road. At the end of this road turn right to follow Cavendish Road to a mini-roundabout. Cross over and turn left on Emmanuel Road alongside Tooting Common for ¼ mile (or enjoy keeping parallel on the grass) then take a tarmac path leading off to the right through a sparse grove of mature trees and under a railway bridge.

Tooting Bec derived its name from ownership of the locality by the Benedictine Abbey of Bec in Normandy. Its near neighbour, Tooting Graveney, recalls the de Gravenel family, remembered also in the River Graveney, a tributary of the Wandle. Both names date back to the time of William the Conqueror, and both have their commons, which combine to form Tooting Common, an area of 221 acres. For centuries locals had grazed their animals here under feudal commoners' rights, but in the 1870s threats of the whole area being smothered with street after street of housing were only narrowly averted when the Metropolitan Board of Works managed to buy the manorial rights, thereby saving the commons for us all to enjoy today.

Follow the tarmac path straight ahead, with only the occasional passing train to disturb the peace, to finally walk alongside the railway and emerge onto Bedford Hill. Cross the road with great care and then turn right over the bridge. Take the tarmac path on the left leading back onto the common, then immediately fork left along a tree-lined gravel path that leads to Tooting Bec Lido.

The café on the Common

Said to be one of the largest swimming pools in the British Isles at 100 yards long and 33 wide, the Lido, which holds one million gallons of water, opened to the public in 1906. Initially the sexes were kept strictly apart and mixed bathing was not introduced until 1931. Hardy souls from the South London swimming club enjoy a dip here throughout the year, even on Christmas Day.

50 yards past the Lido entrance bear right on a gravel track towards a car park, where you head right again along the tree-line to meet a tarmac path. Turn right and follow this path (look out for a lake on the left, hidden by bushes) for nearly half a mile until just before you meet Bedford Hill again, turn left to the San Remo café (which has a customer toilet), then left again to pass the café and follow a tarmac path to Dr Johnson Avenue.

Dr Samuel Johnson, the man who compiled the first comprehensive English dictionary in 1755, liked to visit his friends the Thrales at Thrale Place, which faced Tooting Bec Common. He had an apartment in the house, and used to retire to the summer house to write. Pulled down in 1863, the house and grounds covered 100 acres.

Cross the road, walk past the old keeper's lodge, and after 150 yards turn right on a tarmac path to Elmbourne Road. Cross straight over with care and go ahead along Streathbourne Road. This long street of well-built houses, obviously intended for the better-off, keeps you entertained with a record number of fashionable house names of the day, displayed on terracotta panels, such as Fairycroft, Wintonia, Bryn Glas, and of course Streathbourne. In and around the front doors much original stained glass is still in evidence. When you come to the end of this road turn left to follow Balham High Road for the short distance to Tooting Bec station and the completion of the walk.

Tooting Common

SW18

20 King George's Park

A glimpse of Wandsworth's renowned civic buildings, old brewery, and inns, followed by a parkland stroll in the company of the River Wandle

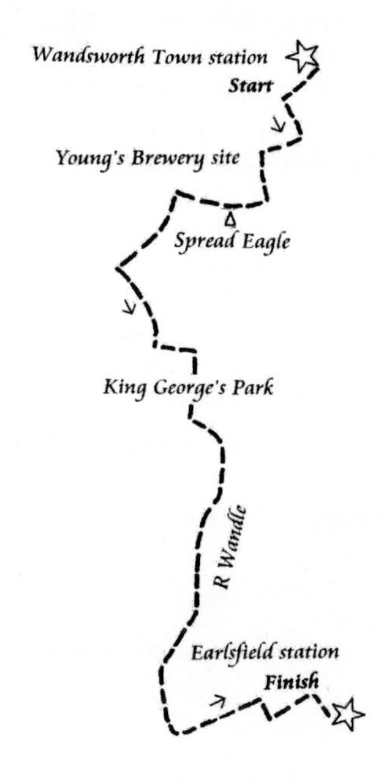

Distance	2½ miles.
Time	1½ hours.
Terrain	Level and paved all the way with two short slopes.
Food and drink	Plenty of choice in Wandsworth and Earlsfield.
Toilets	Wandsworth, Earlsfield.
Start	Wandsworth Town station. Trains to Clapham Junction, Putney etc. Buses 28, 44.
Finish	Earlsfield station. Trains to Clapham Junction, Wimbledon etc. Buses 44, 77, 270.

On leaving Wandsworth Town station, with the Alma pub opposite, turn right to walk past the shops and cafés of Old York Road. Take the second left into Tonsley Hill, then the second right, Tonsley Place. Turn left to cross Fairfield Street at pedestrian lights, then turn left to pass the Town Hall. Bear right into Wandsworth High Street, opposite South Thames College.

The Municipal Buildings, part of the Town Hall complex, were completed in 1937 and display a relief frieze depicting scenes from Wandsworth's rich history. Many Huguenot refugees, fleeing religious persecution in France in the 17th and 18th centuries settled here, and set up industries that contributed greatly to the local prosperity. Mount Nod, the burial ground at the top of East Hill, displays a tablet bearing names of many of them, and their tears are incorporated in the chequered coat of arms of the borough to be seen on the Town Hall.

Carry on past the Town Hall extension (toilet here) and Palace Theatre, with the Spread Eagle opposite.

Opened in 1920, the Wandsworth Palace, one of seven cinemas that have graced the town over the years, closed in 1961 as fashions changed. Later on a stint as a bingo hall, then a gospel church, and now a nightclub, have helped to keep the building alive. Across the road the Spread Eagle, a fine building of 1898, has always been the most important inn in Wandsworth. First mentioned in 1664, it became the principal meeting place for local societies, assemblies, and even church services. It's well worth popping in for a quick drink to admire the authentic interior, which still has much original woodwork, glass, and fittings. Another historic building opposite is the Quaker Meeting House of 1778, the oldest in London. It still retains original panelling, a gallery, and a private burial ground and garden.

The Ram Inn, Wandsworth

Cross Ram Street, where the grand but unused Brewery Tap reminds the passer-by of Young's many years of brewing in the centre of Wandsworth.

A little way along Ram Street, on the brewery wall, is a plaque commemorating the Surrey Iron Railway. Opened in

1803 as the world's first public railway, horses pulled wagons loaded with goods from the Wandle's many mills to a trans-shipment dock near the spot where the river meets the Thames. Running on cast-iron rails, the route eventually extended to quarries at Merstham, but it was never a financial success and closed in 1846.

Keep on ahead to the brewery gates.

Brewing has been carried out on this site since the 16th century, with Young's established here since 1831. Until quite recent years horse-drawn drays delivered beer to their more local pubs (you will see Young's premises as far away as Brighton, and Wiltshire) and their real-ale is still deservedly popular. John Allen Young, the fifth-generation chairman of the firm and a great exponent of traditional brewing died in 2006, the same year that the site was sold for development and operations merged with Charles Wells of Bedford. There is one ray of hope though; among the grand plans for 42 storey tower blocks, 829 residential 'units', shops, and restaurants is the surprising inclusion of a micro-brewery. Look out for a memorial bench to John Young, when you enter King George's Park, which provides a pleasant resting place near the lake.

Go over the Wandle, then cross left at the lights to leave the High Street and continue on the left-hand pavement of Buckhold Road, passing to the right of Southside shopping centre. Cross Neville Gill Close and then rejoice as you leave Wandsworth's traffic behind and go through the gates of King George's Park. Keep right, passing a flourishing oak tree encircled by the memorial bench mentioned earlier.

King George's Park

Partly thanks to a scheme to tackle local unemployment in the 1920s, this park rose from fields and a rubbish dump to become a public park endowed with an ornamental lake, bowling green, playground, and sports facilities. King George V and Queen Mary performed the opening ceremony in 1923, then ten years later the greyhound racing stadium added to the attractions, surviving until the 1960s. Until 1994, a sizeable swimming pool also graced the park.

Now the path takes you past a playground, picnic area, and tennis courts. At a brick-paved crossing path turn left, where you can admire another, and extremely well-equipped playground. At the next junction turn right (there are toilets in the Wandle recreation centre, a few yards ahead) and follow the park's perimeter path. When you come to a ramp and steps keep on ahead on the shared cycle track and footpath, enjoying a glimpse of the fast-flowing Wandle as you progress. Cross Kimber Road and keep on past an adventure centre to trace the riverside once more. Pass a bridge leading to the factories of Bendon Valley, then another that points the way through the distinctive arches of the Henry Prince estate, towards Garratt Lane. Your route, however, forges on ahead, with allotments and school buildings to the right, to skirt through a patch of light woodland. Curving around an open swathe of grass, the path soon arrives at a gate where you leave the park and carry on ahead on Acuba Road.

A grand house called Earlsfield, owned by the Davis family, gave its name to this locality. When the London and South-Western Railway wanted to build a new station here, the house stood in their way. The owners sold up on condition that the name lived on in the station, and the resulting housing that sprang up in the vicinity followed suit. Garratt Lane also gained its name from one house; in the days of Queen Elizabeth I, the Garret, on its own near where the Leather Bottle now stands, formed the lone beginnings of the hamlet of Garratt.

Take the first left, Strathville Road, past terraces of pastel-hued cottages. At a T-junction turn right then left to follow Penwith Road, meeting the Wandle once again. At the junction with Garratt Lane turn right to walk under the bridge and across at the lights to Earlsfield station, and the end of your walk. There are several pubs and cafés within 100 yards, and toilets in the library in Magdalen Road, except Tuesday and Sunday.

SW17, SW18

21 Earlsfield and Tooting

The story of the Mayor of Garratt, followed by a saunter alongside the River Wandle on the way to discover a taste of Tooting

Distance	4¼ miles.
Time	2-2½ hours.
Terrain	One easily-avoided railway footbridge, otherwise level pavements or tarmac except for a ¾ mile stretch of evenly-surfaced gravel riverside path.
Food and drink	Plenty of choice in Earlsfield and Tooting.
Toilets	Earlsfield library (not Tuesday or Sunday), Longmead Road Tooting, or customer toilets in the many cafés and pubs at the start and finish.
Start	Earlsfield station. Trains from Clapham Junction, Wimbledon etc. Buses 44, 77, 270.
Finish	Tooting Broadway station. Northern line, Buses 44, 57, 77, 127, 155, 219, 264, 270, 280, 333, 355, 493, G1.

Turn left out of Earlsfield station, cross Magdalen Road (toilets in library 100 yards along here) and carry on along Garratt Lane, beside the individual shops and cafés that flourish here. On reaching St Andrew's church take the next left into Waynflete Street.

St Andrew's dates from 1891, at a time when local architect EW Mountford busied himself designing many buildings of note, including this one, in the vicinity. Battersea is enriched to this day by Mountford's Town Hall (Battersea Arts Centre), library, and polytechnic, and in central London the Old Bailey is his work.

Carry on past the parish hall and Glebe House, then take the first right, Tranmere Road, which you follow to its end at Burntwood Lane, where you turn right.

Across the road Garratt Green gives every appearance of an unassuming few acres of grass, however in the 18th century this locality played host to the riotous Mayor of Garratt elections, when a bizarre and extraordinary selection of London 'characters' would descend on the green, swear an incomprehensible election oath, and then make a speech, to shouts of approval and general merriment. The assembled crowds, up to 100,000 at the height of the event's popularity, could then choose between such candidates as Squire Blow-me-Down, Lord Twankum, or Sir Harry Dimsdale, the last mayor. Once elected, all and sundry repaired to the Leather Bottle (which you will see in a moment) or one of the dozen or so pubs strung the length of Garratt Lane, which on one notable occasion all ran out of beer, and resorted to selling water at 2d a glass. The first recorded election happened

The Leather Bottle

in 1747, and the last in 1826, with a revival in 1992, when Thomas Rot was beaten by Sir Garibaldi at an 'election' staged at the Leather Bottle.

Press on ahead for ¼ mile to Garratt Lane, which you cross and then turn right. Cross Siward Road (Garratt Park, a tranquil 4-acre verdant haven, hides itself away here) and then pass the Leather Bottle, still a popular watering-hole. Take the next left into Weybourne Street (another park entrance here) and follow the road as it swings right and continues ahead. After passing a couple of side turnings turn left into Trewint Street and cross a bridge over the tree-shaded Wandle.

Before the days of instant power at the flick of a switch, this fast-flowing river powered dozens of mills. In the 1660s James Lloyd's mills were established here, turning saltpetre, charcoal, and sulphur into gunpowder. By 1687 this successful venture had become the second largest producer of gunpowder in England. In later years oil, then paper and bone were processed, with the mill surviving until the end of the 19th century.

Turn left along the riverside path and carry on ahead for ¾ mile, ignoring side turnings, which lead to the industrial environs of Weir Road.

Your nostrils may be assailed by some delicate aromas here, some from the river and some from the surrounding industry, but this will quickly be forgotten as you get into a stride along the riverside. You can rejoice in the lack of traffic, the flora and fauna, and your silent, onward-flowing companion. Later on, at a massive pylon, dense blocks of flats thrust upwards from the former grounds of Wimbledon Football Club.

The Wandle at Earlsfield

When your riverside path ends, traffic lights have been thoughtfully provided to speed you across Plough Lane and on alongside the river, now on its left bank. As you progress, a side-stream diverts you slightly left; this is where the River Graveney, hemmed in by concrete banks, meets the Wandle.

Just occasionally, this half-forgotten little river makes its presence felt, as in the deluge of 16th June 1914 when both the Graveney and the Wandle burst their banks, and submerged Summerstown and Tooting Broadway under six inches of water. The Graveney is named after the de Gravenel family, 11th-century lords of the manor, and can still be seen at various locations, including opposite Waterfall Road, and near Fallsbrook Road. It starts life, as it springs from the hills of south London, as the Norbury Brook.

Keep on ahead under a railway bridge to walk alongside Wandle Meadow nature park. Maintain your direction as you go through a gate to join Chaucer Way. Cross North Road to continue on a footpath beside houses, then turn left to follow Boundary Road, one of the quiet back-streets of Collier's Wood. Keep going to the very end of this road to a footbridge across railway lines (to avoid this, turn right into Briscoe Road, left to cross the railway bridge, then left to rejoin the walk in Blackshaw Road). Once across, follow a wide passageway which leads over Kenlor Road to emerge on Blackshaw Road, opposite St George's Hospital. Cross this road with care, using the central refuge 50 yards to your left if necessary, then turn right. Pass the hospital car park and turn left to follow Maybury Street. Press on to the brick-wall end of the street, where a passageway with the rustic title of Common Field Lane leads through to Effort Street. Straightaway turn right to follow Tooting Grove, a street lined with 1930s flats, and a green-pantiled pub of the period, the Little House. At the end turn left to follow Tooting High Street.

The confluence of Wandle and Graveney

To your right is another distinctive hostelry, the Trafalgar Arms, still advertising long-forgotten Hodgsons' Kingston Stout, while the next street you cross is Recovery Street, so well-placed right by the hospital.

Cross at the pedestrian lights and turn left to forge on towards Tooting Broadway, passing some old houses, set back from the road. At the Tube station turn right into Mitcham Road (don't worry, in a few minutes you will return here, the end of your walk, after a diversion to the famous Granada, and the covered markets). Pass Babosh, a modern café providing food, drink, and a customer toilet for the weary walker. Keep going until you spy the Gala Bingo Hall, where you cross at the lights.

Look back to the former Granada cinema, which opened in 1931.

Tooting Broadway's splendid lamp-and-signpost

Designed to seat 4000, and housing the 'Mighty Wurlitzer' organ, the first film to be screened here was 'Monte Carlo' starring Jeanette MacDonald and Jack Buchanan. The cathedral-like interior featured Gothic decorations, stained-glass windows and a marbled and mirrored foyer. Thankfully, a threatened demolition was averted when the building achieved Grade I listing, the first of any cinema.

Turn left to traverse the other side of this busy shopping street until you come to Longmead Road, which doubles as a bus terminus. Turn right here, following Longmead Road as it snakes to the left, then look out for an entrance to Broadway Market, into which you turn (if the markets are closed, simply continue to Totterdown Street, turn left, then left again at the High Street). Wend your way through the cluster of stalls, among which are haberdashers, butchers, a couple of cafés, world food stalls, a seller of old, polished tools, knobs, and knockers, and even an astrologer, to finally emerge at Tooting High Street. Turn left for 100 yards to the welcome sight of King Edward VII on his plinth, marking journey's end for you.

The former Granada cinema, Tooting

SW16

22 Streatham

Some unexpected historical discoveries in this busy town, then an escape to gardens, grass, and birdsong at Streatham Common and the Rookery

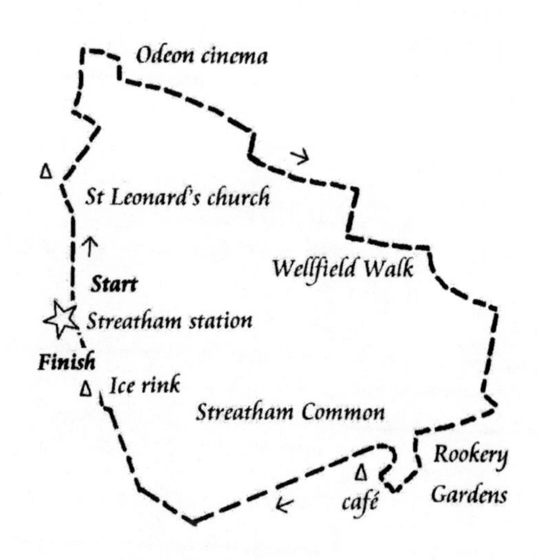

Distance	3 miles.
Time	1½ hours.
Terrain	Pavements or tarmac paths all the way. Several steep slopes, and some steps, which can be avoided.
Food and drink	Cafés and pubs in Streatham High Road, a delicatessen in Sunnyhill Road, and the San Remo café by the Rookery gardens.
Toilets	Streatham station (in the waiting room on platform 1), Streatham library, the Rookery, Streatham Common.
Start and Finish	Streatham station. Trains to West Croydon, Wimbledon etc. Buses 50, 109, 118, 159, 249, 250, 255, G1, P13.

From Streatham station turn left along Streatham High Road. Carry on ahead, crossing Gleneagle Road, 100 yards after which you climb a few steps to walk diagonally right across Streatham Green. To avoid the steps, carry on to the road junction to rejoin the walk.

This is a remnant of the ancient village centre of Streatham, and used to possess a row of 300 year-old elm trees. It was also a favourite place for children to play cricket, using a tree as a wicket; if the ball ended up in the main road, rolling off downhill, it counted as a six. The Dyce fountain used to stand at the nearby road junction, and was fed from a tank in the churchyard, where the local youngsters could indulge in a bit of sport by turning the water on and off, thereby catching a thirsty and unsuspecting passer-by with a sudden, soaking jet. The fountain was designed in 1862 by William Dyce, churchwarden of St Leonard's church, a member of the Royal Academy, and a leading Pre-Raphaelite artist. He also planned the chancel for St Leonard's.

Dyce Memorial Fountain, Streatham Green

Pass the Dyce fountain and turn right at Mitcham Lane, then walk to the traffic lights, cross to St Leonard's church and turn right.

On your left is the Roman Catholic Church of the English Martyrs, completed in 1893. The superbly ornate interior, with a fine altar, stained glass, and rich carved decoration, is topped by a tower and spire nearly 137ft high; 9ft higher than its neighbour, St Leonard's, the parish church. Mentioned as a chapel in the Domesday Book of 1086, St Leonard's was rebuilt c1350, and the lower part of the tower is from this time. In 1778, and again in 1831, rebuilding took place, then in 1863 the chancel was added. Fire ravaged the building on the evening of May 5th 1975, but thankfully spared some of the fine memorials within, including the sumptuous Howland monument in the tower, the Thrale memorials to Streatham's renowned family of brewers, a 14th-century effigy of Sir John Ward, and a wordy inscription to Edmund Tylney, Master of the Revels to Queen Elizabeth I and King James I. Occasionally tours of the crypt take place; there you can see the family vaults, and ancient, cobweb-draped coffins, of Streatham families of long ago.

Continue along the High Road then take the first turning on the left, Prentis Road. Pass the Liberal synagogue and on the other side of the road the Royal Mail office, which sports a splendid royal coat of arms above the entrance. Take the first right, Ockley Road, along which is an interesting group of houses in the art nouveau style, notably 'The Garden' at number 9. Turn first right along Becmead Avenue to meet the High Road opposite the Odeon cinema.

St Leonard's church

The Odeon started life as the Astoria cinema, with over 2,500 eager customers arriving for the opening ceremony on 30th June 1930. They were treated to 'Paris', a colour 'talkie' film starring Jack Buchanan, and live acts including 'The Peculiar Pair' and Teddy Brown on the xylophone. The cinema was re-named the Odeon in 1961, and today sports a total of 8 screens.

Cross over the main road and turn right to pass the green-domed library.

Sir Henry Tate of Tate & Lyle fame, one of Streatham's most illustrious residents, presented the library to the people of Streatham. He lived at Park Hill, right at the top of Streatham Common, and endowed many other public buildings including Brixton library, outside which is a bust of Sir Henry with an inscription affirming that he was an 'upright merchant' and 'wise philanthropist'. He also benefited the nation by bringing us not only the Tate

Gallery, but also the humble sugar cube. The library opened in 1890, with the crown-topped clock appearing in 1912 as a memorial to King Edward VII.

Turn first left to follow Pinfold Road, which after passing Farm Avenue becomes Angles Road. Follow this road as it swings to the right, then turn left at Sunnyhill Road. The opportunity for a baguette and drink presents itself on your downhill stroll, at Le Tour de France delicatessen. At the T-junction with Valley Road cross the road by using the zebra crossing a few yards to the left, then turn right.

The fame of Streatham's wells and springs stretched far and wide in days gone by. In the High Road stood the Pump House, from where fresh spring water straight from the pump used to be delivered by the village postman at 1d for three buckets, and on Streatham Common mineral wells were discovered, with Streatham Spa becoming hugely popular in the early 18th century. These purgative waters were claimed to cure any number of afflictions including gout, jaundice, and bilious attacks, and are said to have caused the local locksmith, who was quite ill, to pass four worms, one of which measured eight foot three inches long. The principal spa was at the Rookery, which you will visit later on in the walk, while a little to your left in Valley Road the Well House dispensed the waters from 1793 until a wartime bomb destroyed the pump house in 1942.

Pass Well Close and then after a few yards, opposite the end of Wellfield Road turn left on a steeply-climbing tarmac slope, Wellfield Walk. At the top turn right on Springwell Road, where you can begin to enjoy the benefit of your steep climb as a wide vista opens out before you. Turn left, uphill again, on Valleyfield Road, passing a rustic cottage on the corner of Benhurst Lane, followed by a solidly-built house, with a fine iron veranda, bearing the date 1882. Turn right at Leigham Court Road, which has three or four more of these good Victorian houses of the 1880s. At Streatham Common North use the pedestrian lights to cross straight ahead to the Common, turn left and then after 20 yards turn right on a tarmac path. This soon meets a crossing path, where you turn right and continue through a long woodland clearing to arrive at a car park, which you cut across to the left, to an avenue of hornbeams and a gate in the fence of the Rookery gardens. Go through this gate to where an orderly line of wooden benches are perfectly placed to best appreciate the delightful garden scene.

In 1659 a group of thirsty farm workers slaked their thirst at a spring here, discovering the effects of mineral water in the process. Later on, word of the curative powers of these waters spread, and in time three wells were in operation at this spot, visited by an enthusiastic public, whose carriages used to queue along the High Road for a mile to enter the spa. By the late 1700s the waters had become contaminated and were said to 'smell strongly like boiled eggs' so that eventually just one well survived as the 'wishing' well,

Streatham's last remaining well, Rookery Gardens

which is still there, in the formal garden. For many years a mansion, The Rookery, stood here, and after being purchased by the London County Council the grounds were opened to the public in 1913.

Turn left, downhill, to walk through the superb formal garden, then branch left again to chance upon a green field, the Orchard, laid out with picnic tables. Climb back up to pass a neat wooden shelter, a gift from Stenton Covington, the driving force behind the campaign to save the Rookery from housing development in the early 1900s. When you are ready to leave the gardens go through the gate and turn left to the San Remo café, and toilets. Opposite the café cross Streatham Common South and follow the descending tarmac path beside a line of London plane trees.

Doctor Samuel Johnson's favourite walk led from the house of his friends at Streatham Park, the Thrales, to the top of Streatham Common, down the field-path to Norbury, then back home again. That was in the 18th century, and since then the common has changed from being a source of fuel and animal grazing ground for the commoners to a public open space. The lofty heights, which served as a location for one of a line of beacon fires lit to celebrate Queen Victoria's 1887 Jubilee, also give fine views towards the distant wooded Surrey hills. Today Streatham Common offers acres of grass and woodland, viewpoints, a playground, an annual Fun Dog show, Kite day, Funfair, and even Shakespeare in the Rookery.

At a crossing path carry straight on, then as your path levels out bear right to converge on the main road opposite Greyhound Lane (toilets to the right). Keep on along the tree-lined edge of the Common to cross the junction with Streatham Common North, and then by the war memorial gardens go left across the High Road and turn right. Very soon you will pass a go-kart track housed in the old Streatham bus garage and the famous Streatham ice rink to arrive back at Streatham station, and walk's end.

Streatham Common

SW16

23 Norbury

Linked by a thread of quiet residential roads, three delightful green spaces, each with its own unique appeal, are the focus of this walk

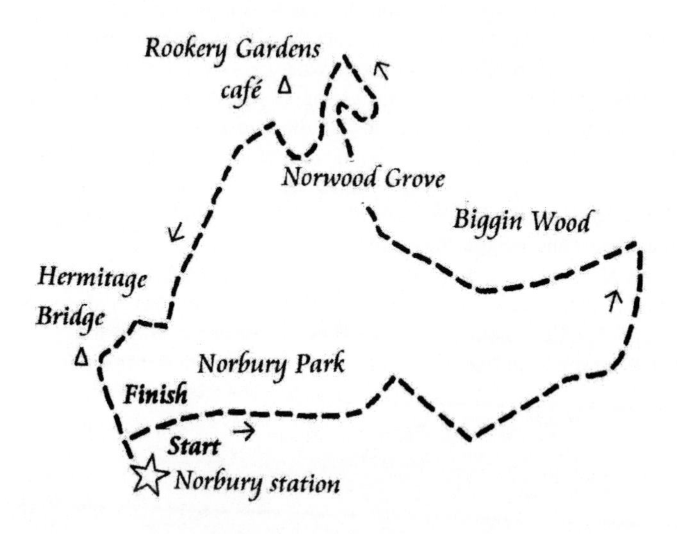

Distance	3¼ miles.
Time	1½ hours.
Terrain	Pavements, tarmac paths, and grass, on fairly gentle gradients.
Food and drink	Norbury has two or three cafés, but the best choice may be the San Remo café at the Rookery, near the half-way point.
Toilets	Norbury, Norwood Grove.
Start and Finish	Norbury station. Trains to West Croydon, Clapham Junction, etc. Buses 50, 109, 255. Bus 250 stops nearby in Green Lane.

From Norbury station follow signs for Norbury Park. Cross Norbury Avenue to turn right into the park (toilet here) then take the right-hand path to strike out along an avenue of young trees, with the twin transmission masts of Crystal Palace and Norwood firmly in your sights.

Croydon Corporation bought land that had previously been the North Surrey golf course in 1935 to create Norbury Park, which before about 1920 had been open fields. To your left the park is bounded by the Norbury Brook, a small watercourse that takes on the title of the River Graveney at nearby Hermitage Bridge, which you cross near the end of your walk.

Branch right at the next junction of paths, then keep on ahead to pass a play area and emerge on Green Lane, opposite Norbury Hill. Cross with care and turn right, then after 300 yards turn left into St Oswald's Road, with a church of the same name on the corner. Press on along this road, gradually climbing to reach a roundabout, where you fork left along Biggin Hill. The gradient becomes more challenging as you cross Covington Way and continue past a terrace of houses, at the end of which, almost opposite Marston Way, respite comes as you turn left along a wide tarmac footpath to pass tennis courts and a Capital Ring signpost. Your route coincides with this 78-mile circular walk for the next mile or so, as far as Norwood Grove. Keep on ahead to enter Biggin Wood.

This pleasant piece of woodland, acquired for the public to enjoy in 1939, is part of the ancient Great North Wood, an extensive stretch of woods that once covered the slopes and hills of the whole of the north of Surrey. The Northwood, a large tract of this forest north of Croydon that eventually suc-

Biggin Wood

cumbed to Victorian house builders, is remembered in the name Norwood. Said to contain only oak trees, it stretched to over 800 acres when in the 17th century the Archbishop of Canterbury was forced to relinquish the wood to Oliver Cromwell. In later years Mr James Epps, who lived in a big old house here, had to leave during the month of May owing to sleepless nights caused by the song of the nightingale, and to this day springtime brings the wood to life with birdsong.

Follow this path as it snakes through and eventually out of the wood. Back on the road again, bear right on Covington Way to cross straight over Norbury Hill and descend to Gibson's Hill and a gateway to the parkland of Norwood Grove. Go through the gate and follow the rising path to walk through a patch of light woodland and enter the enclosed gardens. Go left to follow the low metal fence, then keep on ahead through a circular rose arbour and carry on towards the White House (there are toilets ahead, on the right).

Norwood Grove, the White House, has had several illustrious residents, including Arthur Anderson and his wife Margaret, who took the house in 1847. He came from humble beginnings in the Shetland Isles, went to sea at the age of 11, worked later as a clerk, on a daily ration of twopennyworth of bread and cheese and a pint of porter, and eventually rose to become joint founder of the P & O shipping line. From 1878 to 1913 Mr and Mrs Frederick Nettlefold lived here. In 1833, at the age of 16, Frederick had joined his father's iron and screw business, which within a few years became the first major factory in the world to produce woodscrews on automatic machinery. In time the firm became Guest, Keen, and Nettlefold, a leading engineering company well-known as GKN.

Norwood Grove

Both the house and its grounds might have been obliterated by bricks and mortar had it not been for local resident Stenton Covington, who managed to form a committee to raise the funds required to buy the estate when it came up for sale in 1924. The money was duly raised, and Norwood Grove, house and grounds, were opened for public enjoyment by the Prince of Wales in November 1926.

Walk past the front of the house (note the blue plaque in memory of Mr and Mrs Nettlefold), stroll round to the left past the orangery and under a cedar tree, then leave the gardens and park by turning left onto a vehicle-wide tarmac track known as Copgate Path. Pass the back of the house, go past a barrier, and continue along the fence-lined path towards a solitary old lodge-house.

The Lodge, a Victorian building once occupied by Stenton Covington, stands near to the gate pillars of the old carriage drive to Norwood Grove. The dip here, crossing a ditch with a trickle of water in wet weather, marks the ancient boundary between the parishes of Streatham and Croydon, and still forms the line between the London boroughs of Croydon and Lambeth. You may spot an old boundary marker, one of several, if you peep over the bridge. If the attractions of the San Remo café and the beautiful Rookery gardens appeal to you at this point, just keep on along the track, past the lodge, and you'll be there in five minutes.

Just before the lodge turn left through a gateway and go diagonally left across the grass on a well-trodden trail which brings you back to a corner of the low fence you met earlier. Branch to the right here along a tarmac path beside a line of trees, with a broad sweep of wooded suburbia in view, then keep on ahead, and then right, on a faint path across the grassy slope to a gate where you leave the park once more and turn right on Covington Way. Take the first left, Briar Avenue, a leafy thoroughfare which you follow all the way to a T-junction with Green Lane, where you cross, turn right, and then take the second left, signed Norbury station, on an un-named road past a supermarket. Turn left to follow Streatham High Road, crossing the inconspicuous Hermitage Bridge, where the road becomes London Road, Norbury.

At this spot, on the borough boundary, the Norbury Brook becomes the River Graveney, a tributary of the Wandle. The bridge parapet across the road indicates an open stretch of river, which then dips in and out of culverts on its traverse through Tooting. The name Graveney stems from the de Gravenel family, lords of the manor in the 11th century. Hermitage Bridge is named after an ancient hermit's cell nearby, where Richard Adams, 'Ye Hermite', lived and died in 1545.

Carry on past the police station to Norbury station, where the walk ends.

24 Colliers Wood and Morden Hall Park

Wandle Park, Deen City Farm (all the farm animals you could wish for, including horses) riverside and parkland walking, historical interest, shops, stalls, food and drink at Merton Abbey Mills

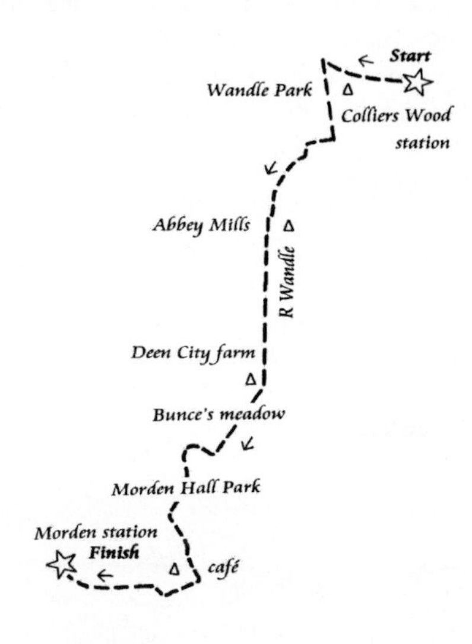

Distance	2½ miles.
Time	1-1½ hours.
Terrain	Level gravel paths and pavements.
Food and drink	Café and pub at Merton Abbey Mills, cafés at Deen City Farm and Morden Hall Park.
Toilets	At the three venues above.
Start	Colliers Wood station. Northern line, Buses 57, 131, 152, 200, 219, 470, 493.
Finish	Morden station. Northern line, Buses 80, 93, 118, 154, 157, 163, 164, 201, 293, 413, 470, K5.

Commencing at Colliers Wood station, cross the High Street, turn left, then immediately right into Baltic Close. At the end of this short cul-de-sac go through a gate into Wandle Park and follow the path ahead to cross a footbridge over a wide, shallow, plant-filled waterway. Cross another reed-fringed bridge to pass a drinking fountain. There is a children's playground away to the right.

Opened in 1907, 11-acre Wandle Park occupies the site of the millpond of Merton Corn Mill, which was owned by James Perry, a friend of Lord Nelson. There were numerous mills along the River Wandle, and although most of these old industrial buildings have vanished you will see some survivors on this walk; glance to the right as you cross the river to spot the former Connolly's Leather Works.

Keep left to leave the park and cross a footbridge over the fast-flowing river, then turn left along Wandle Bank. As you progress you will pass Bank Buildings, a grand title for this charming row of Georgian cottages. Turn right at the main road, walk past the bus garage, then cross at pedestrian lights towards the superstore. Turn right before the blue bridge to walk alongside the Wandle again.

At this spot William Morris established his print works in 1881, producing tapestry, carpets, printed and woven fabrics, and stained glass in his unique 'Arts and Crafts' style, utilising free-flowing designs inspired by nature. Morris & Co designs are still popular to this day.

Keep on beside the river to emerge at Station Road. Turn right then immediately left, through an arch, cross Merantun Way, then carry on ahead with the river to your left.

The Wandle at Abbey Mills

Across the bridge are the historic buildings of Merton Abbey Mills, the former printing works of famous fabric designers Liberty & Co. Originally Merton Priory stood here. It had been established in 1117 by Augustinian monks and became one of the wealthiest monastic houses in England, but fell foul of Henry VIII in the Reformation and ended up being plundered for stone to build Nonsuch Palace. Nowadays you can enjoy craft fairs, entertainments of all sorts, food, drink, and displays of industrial heritage here, including an original water-wheel, restored and providing power for the resident potter.

Press on ahead to cross Windsor Avenue and continue along the road to Deen City Farm.

Pigs, sheep, cows, chickens; they're all here to delight the children, and if you're lucky you may see horses exercising in the ring. The farm has a café and toilets, is free to enter, and is open Tuesday–Sunday and Bank Holidays 10-4.30.

Deen City Farm

Maintaining your direction beside the river, take the path to the left of the farm entrance signed 'Wandle Trail Morden Hall Park'. This path through Bunce's Meadow continues alongside the Wandle, eventually swinging to the right, then across a ditch, where you turn left to cross Tramlink tracks. You are now in Morden Hall Park, a National Trust property. Take the first left turn to enter the 'wetlands', an area of water-loving trees and plants.

Willows, alders, and reeds thrive in this flood plain, while other parts of the park are given over to meadow, nowadays cut for hay but until the 1970s grazed by cattle. Mature trees and woodland add to the countryside feel of the park, a rare survivor in this suburban setting.

Follow the path through the wetlands, then across a wooden footbridge, after which you bear left across two more bridges to arrive at an elegant white arch bridge, spanning the main river. This is a favourite place for youngsters to splash about in summer. Do not cross the bridge, instead keep on alongside the river to reach the Snuff Mill environmental centre, Morden Cottage, and the Rose Garden.

Snuff, made from dried and ground-up tobacco at this rustic mill, provided the funds for the creation of Morden Hall Park. Owned by the Hatfeild family, the mill continued to operate until 1922, then in 1941 local philanthropist Gilliat Hatfeild died and left the estate to the careful management of the National Trust.

Turn right at the Snuff Mill, cross a gushing side-stream, then go left to locate the café, garden centre, and toilets. Cross the bridge into the car park and immediately turn right to leave the park through a pedestrian gate. Turn right along Morden Hall Road, cross at the lights and take the road facing you, Aberconway Road, for 300 yards to the end of the walk at Morden station, for Northern line and buses.

Morden Hall Park

SW19, SW20

25 Merton Park

A few reminders of Merton's most famous resident, Lord Nelson, followed by a stroll through the 'Garden Suburb' created by John Innes

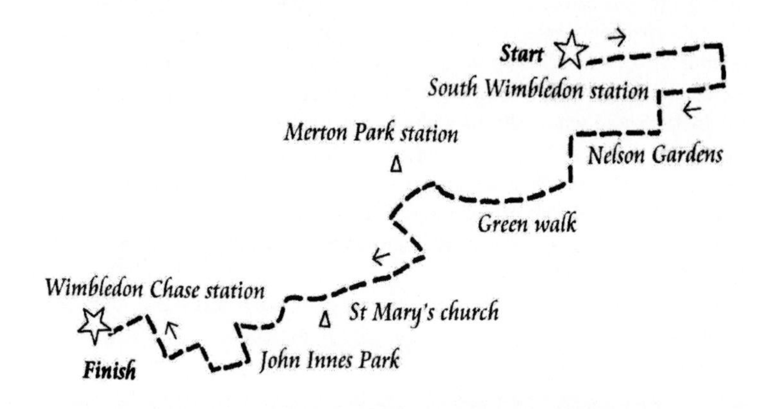

Distance	2¼ miles.
Time	1-1½ hours.
Terrain	One long gravel track which can get quite muddy, otherwise reasonably level tarmac and pavements.
Food and drink	Both South Wimbledon and Wimbledon Chase offer one or two pubs and cafés.
Toilets	John Innes Park.
Start	South Wimbledon station. Northern line, Buses 57, 93, 131, 152, 219.
Finish	Wimbledon Chase station. Trains to Wimbledon, Sutton etc., Buses 152, 163, 164.

Turn right on leaving South Wimbledon station and walk along Merton High Street, crossing Pincott Road. Shortly after the traffic lights at Haydons Road turn right at the Nelson Arms to follow Abbey Road. When you come to the Princess Royal pub turn right along Nelson Grove Road.

The Nelson Arms marks the site of the entrance to Admiral Lord Nelson's estate at Merton Place, where in the company of the vivacious Emma Hamilton and her elderly husband Sir William Hamilton, Nelson enjoyed some respite at 'Paradise Merton' from his famous seafaring exploits. Their gardens and grounds, with uninterrupted views across fields to Wimbledon Hill, extended across Merton High Street, underneath which ran a brick tunnel linking the two halves of the estate. In front of the house stretched an ornamental expanse of water, referred to as 'The Nile' after one of Nelson's most famous victories. Nelson and Emma lived at Merton Place from 1801 (Sir William died in 1803) until the great admiral's demise at the Battle of Trafalgar in 1805, and within 20 years the house had been sold and development of the estate began. All trace of this romantic location has now vanished, but the names of Nelson, Emma Hamilton, and Trafalgar are still much in evidence in local street and pub names. As you stroll along Nelson Grove Road, you may notice a block of flats named Merton Place, occupying the spot where the old house stood.

Very soon you meet Pincott Road again; turn left here, then right to follow High Path, with the Trafalgar pub on the corner.

Admiral Lord Nelson remembered in Merton: at the Trafalgar, and the Nelson Arms

A lone survivor of the 1950s slum clearance that gave way to the High Path estate, the Trafalgar is Merton's smallest pub, serves real ale, offers jazz on Sundays, and prides itself on being the oldest free house in the locality. A little further along High Path, the church of St John's, built to commemorate the centenary of Nelson's death, dates from 1914. Contained within is an altarpiece made of timber from HMS Victory, and stained glass by Burne-Jones. Nelson Gardens, opened here on land given by a family member as a memorial to Lord Nelson, sports a pair of 12-pounder guns, said to have been a feature of Merton Place.

Carry on past St John's church and Nelson Gardens, then cross Morden Road at the pedestrian lights and turn left. Follow this busy main road past some warehouses until just before a recreation ground turn right through a gate to follow a tree-lined gravel track (in wet weather you can avoid some squelching along here by taking the parallel tarmac path on your left, rejoining through a hedge gap further on).

This 'Green Walk' formed the track of a loop line from Tooting to Wimbledon via Merton Abbey, linking with an existing line to West Croydon at Merton Park, which had a station (at first called 'Lower Merton') from 1858. Passenger trains ceased in 1929, although a dwindling freight service continued until 1975. There still remains a fragment of the original platform in the undergrowth next to a newly-built terrace of houses, and the spruced-up Victorian station house is now a private dwelling. The frequent and well-used trams that rush to and from Croydon today are a far cry from the elderly rolling stock that used to rattle sporadically along these lines in the 1980s. Some years ago this path through the trees nearly became a major road linking up with Merantun Way, until a madcap scheme to tunnel under Kingston Road level crossing received the thumbs down.

Eventually you will meet a crossing path; turn left here, cross the Tramlink tracks, and walk along a path between houses to emerge in Dorset Road.

Now you enter the holly-hedged Merton Park estate, the 'Original Garden Suburb', created by John Innes, successful City developer, and his architect EG Quartermain. The fields on which they laid out roads and houses from 1867 onwards extended as far as Lower Morden, and the differing styles of building apparent in Merton Park are partly due to the length of time it took to develop those parts that were not within walking distance of Wimbledon station. Quartermain designed many houses of character, and several public buildings, in the locality. He died in 1904, the same year as John Innes. Fortunately a young local architect, JS Brocklesby, then continued the tradition of stylish building with quality materials that makes the area so popular today.

Turn left along Dorset Road, cross with care to continue on the right-hand pavement, then take the first right turn, Melrose Road. As you stroll along this road look out for an interesting selection of 'Arts and Crafts' style cottages, designed by Brocklesby between 1906-11, and blessed with unusually long and well-kept front gardens. Keep on ahead to the war memorial and St Mary's church.

Gilbert, Sheriff of Surrey and founder of Merton Priory, commenced the building of St Mary's in 1114. Norman parts of the church still remain, alongside an early 13 chancel and a fine roof dating from 1400. Memorials in the church include an alabaster monument of 1597 to Gregory Lovell, 'cofferer' (treasurer) to the household of Queen Elizabeth, several 'hatchments' which would have been hung outside the house of a deceased person of importance and include those of Lord Nelson and Sir William Hamilton, and stained glass windows by Morris & Co commemorating John Innes. Another interesting relic is 'Nelson's Seat', said to have been used by the admiral in his box-pew. Between the church and vicarage stands a Norman arch of c1175, once part of the Priory, discovered when the old Abbey House

St Mary's church

was knocked down to make way for Liberty's print works in 1914 and rebuilt here in 1935. Until John Innes started developing Merton Park in the late 19th century St Mary's would have been surrounded by fields and farms, its nearest neighbour being 17th-century Church House, reminders of which are the ancient red-brick wall and fine wrought-iron gate opposite the church. The tomb of John Innes, garlanded with swags and cherubs, can be found in the churchyard.

Norman archway at St Mary's church

Carry on past the church along the narrowing Church Path, which continues past the church hall and a row of old cottages, to meet Mostyn Road. Cross with care straight over and go through a gate on the left into John Innes Park. Follow the path as it swings right past a bowling green (there are some rather superior Arts and Crafts toilets to the left, through an arch) then turn left opposite a rockery to pass a fishpond encircled with low railings, aiming for a hedge gap which leads you to the Bandstand.

The garden of John Innes' home at the Manor House (now part of Rutlish School) became John Innes Park after being bequeathed to the people of Merton in his will. As well as being a delightful place to enjoy a stroll, the park offers tennis courts, bowling, and an annual Music in the Park concert, and achieved a prestigious Green Flag award in 2009. Apart from the pleasant environs of Merton Park John Innes also left his mark with the founding in 1910 of the John Innes Horticultural Institution, the first centre for research into genetics and plant breeding in the country, which is now based in Norwich.

Pass to the right of the bandstand and turn right on a path between the buildings of Rutlish School. Shortly you will arrive at a recreation ground, where you turn right on the perimeter path and then after a left-hand bend leave through a gate into Watery Lane. Turn left to follow Manor Road, then go right at Cannon Hill Lane, and left at Kingston Road. Your walk ends here, at Wimbledon Chase, where you can cross at the lights for train or bus services to Wimbledon, or carry on under the bridge for a café, passing the recently-closed Emma Hamilton pub, a last reminder of the enduring popularity of the story of Nelson and Lady Hamilton.

The Bandstand, John Innes Park

SW20

26 West Wimbledon

Keep fit on this uphill walk, and enjoy the peaceful Holland Garden, a playground at Cottenham Park, and then a break at Maher's café and bakery

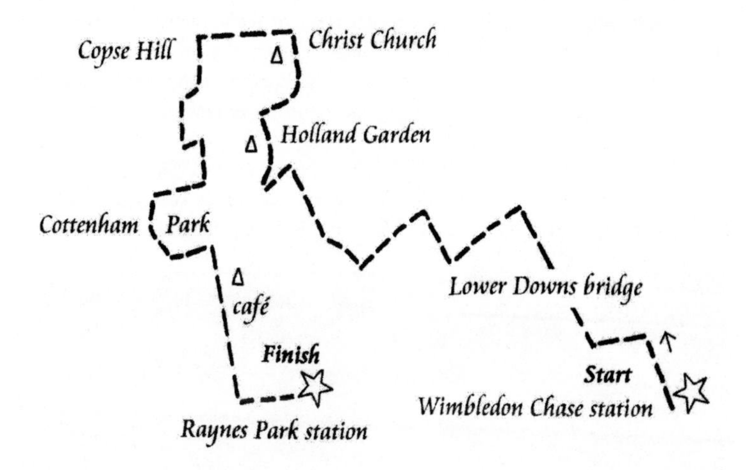

Distance	2¾ miles.
Time	1½ hours.
Terrain	Tarmac or pavements, with two fairly steep gradients.
Food and drink	Wimbledon Chase and Raynes Park.
Toilets	Cottenham Park.
Start	Wimbledon Chase station. Trains to Wimbledon, Sutton etc. Buses 152, 163, 164.
Finish	Raynes Park station. Trains to Wimbledon, Clapham Junction, Surbiton etc. Buses 57, 131, 152, 163, 200.

Turn right on leaving Wimbledon Chase station and walk under the bridge, then straightaway turn right into Chase Side Avenue and continue to the end of this quiet cul-de-sac. Turn left along The Chase, a wide grassy strip with a footpath and cycle track, and carry on to a road junction.

The Chase follows the route of a major water main, opened by the Lambeth Water Company in 1850 and running ten miles, from their works at Thames Ditton (and later from Staines reservoir) via Raynes Park and South Wimbledon to a reservoir at Brixton. Over the years there have been a couple of burst pipes, once where you are now standing, and another in a back garden near Merton Park, both of which unleashed a torrent of water sufficient to rapidly engulf the surrounding streets to a depth of six inches or more.

Turn right here to follow Lower Downs Road (not sharp right into Burstow Road) and press on under 7'9" high Lower Downs railway bridge, a notorious obstacle for over height vehicles that strike, or wedge themselves in, this extra-low aperture. Continue to a set of traffic lights, crossing with great care at one of the road narrowings to gain the left-hand pavement, and turn left along Worple Road. At a set of pedestrian lights cross over and maintain the same direction on the right-hand pavement, to take the next right turn, Arterberry Road.

In the 1870s a rough track from Wimbledon known as Walpole Lane came to an end some way before Raynes Park, which had to be reached by a footpath threading across fields. Soon after this housing development began in

Holland Garden

earnest, aided by the popularity of the All England lawn tennis championships, which were staged in a field near the railway line from 1877 until the club moved to Church Road in 1922. Eventually Worple Road, the through route to Raynes Park, became a reality, with the opening in 1891 accompanied by a brass band and much ceremony. Also laid out in the late 1800s, Arterberry Road's zig-zag course, unlike most of the fairly straight roads that climb to the Ridgway, was planned for the benefit of horses, to make the steep climb less arduous.

After 175 yards turn left to walk the length of Montana Road, then turn right into Langham Road, cross Devas Road (named after Thomas Devas, 19th-century owner of the estate on which these houses were built), and go right again on Pepys Road. Keep on uphill, crossing to the left hand side with care, then turn left along Cambridge Road. Cross over to enter Holland Garden through a gate at the end of the railings, from where you trace the ascending path to the right.

Holland Garden, an unexpected delight in this residential area, had been a field belonging to the Holland family who lived higher up the hill at 'Holmhurst'. Lady Holland gave the garden to the Council in 1928 in memory of her husband, the head of a shipping line, Justice of the Peace, and mayor of Wimbledon in 1906.

Climb to the top of the gardens and leave through a gate onto Cottenham Park Road. Cross over and turn right, uphill. Keep on ahead as the road swings to the left, to arrive at Christ Church.

Opened as a chapel-of-ease to St Mary's, Wimbledon in 1859, Christ Church had to wait until 1961 to gain its own parish. Designed by SS Teulon, architect of the Wimbledon Village Club and other notable local buildings, the main body of the church is of Kentish ragstone. Planned originally to accommodate the growing population brought about by the opening of the railway from Nine Elms to Woking in 1838, the church has been extended and improved over the years, and possesses many fine interior features, including a decorated hammer-beam roof.

Turn left to follow Copse Hill, where some of the original Victorian mansions are still in place, then after passing High Cedar Drive take the next left, Cottenham Drive. Follow this road steeply downhill, with glimpses of a far-reaching southward prospect above the rooftops, until you meet Cottenham Park Road again. Turn left here, then right at Durham Road, and first right at Melbury Gardens. Follow this road for 150 yards before crossing over to enter Cottenham Park. There are toilets here.

Charles Pepys, first Earl of Cottenham, gave his name to this locality when he moved to Prospect Place, a 250-acre estate between Copse Hill and Coombe Lane with gardens landscaped by Humphry Repton, in 1831. He was descended from John Pepys of Cottenham, a village near Cambridge. Hoping

Christ Church

for some peace and respite from his important role as an MP and later Lord Chancellor, for himself, his wife, and fifteen children, he understandably refused to sell any of his land when plans for the new railway, which would have seriously encroached on his estate, were announced shortly after he moved in. This meant the line had to be built on the 'lowlands' south of Worple Road, requiring the embankment that we see today. Charles Pepys died in 1851, and his estate ended up being sold for development, including most notably the Atkinson Morley convalescent home of St George's Hospital, which opened in 1869.

Keep to the left through this small but pleasant green space, past a playground, and then turn left to leave the park through a gate onto Cambridge Road. Turn left, then right at Durham Road, where you will soon spot the welcome sight of Maher's bakery and café. Keep on to the end of Durham Road, where you turn left to the centre of Raynes Park, named after local 19th landowner Edward Rayne. The walk ends here, with a choice of trains to Wimbledon, Clapham Junction, Surbiton etc. or buses to Kingston, New Malden, and Wimbledon.

SW19

27 Wimbledon

An introduction to bustling Wimbledon Village and the familiar church spire seen by millions of tennis fans, with Wimbledon Park's lake, playground, and gardens as a relaxing contrast

Distance	3 miles
Time	1½ hours.
Terrain	Pavements or tarmac, with one steep hill.
Food and drink	Plenty of choice at the beginning and end of the walk, plus a café in Wimbledon Park.
Toilets	Wimbledon Centre Court shopping centre, Wimbledon Park, Southfields.
Start	Wimbledon station. Trains to Clapham Junction, Surbiton, Sutton etc. District line, Buses 57, 93, 131, 156, 163, 164, 200, 219, 493.
Finish	Southfields station. District line, Buses 39, 493.

From Wimbledon station turn right towards Wimbledon Hill Road. Cross Alexandra Road, then at Ely's department store turn left to follow Worple Road.

'New Wimbledon' (in deference to the much older village up the hill) still had a few fields, farms, and country lanes lingering on when Joseph Ely commenced trading in 1876, and very soon the newly-named 'Ely's Corner', along with a diverse range of retail outlets advertising their wares in the uninhibited style of the day, made the town a popular place to shop. More expansion occurred following the opening of several important new rail connections, to West Croydon, Epsom, Kingston, and London Bridge, from 'Wimbledon and Merton' station as it then was. Some of the original buildings are still with us today, notably the Prince of Wales pub, built in 1870, and the Wimbledon Theatre, which opened in 1910. In Queen's Road the preserved Baptist church and Fire Station facades, and the 1930s Town Hall are reminders of how the town used to look.

Once past the shops cross at pedestrian lights to continue on the right-hand pavement, going straight ahead at a roundabout. Take the next right, Malcolm Road, and at the end of this cul-de-sac follow Sunnyside Passage, climbing steeply, to emerge in Sunnyside. Carry on ahead for 125 yards, then just after house number 20 take a short path on the right leading through to Oldfield Road. Take a moment to admire a row of 200 year-old cottages, set back behind proper little cottage gardens, before you come to the busy Ridgway, where you turn right.

Across the road is the Village Club and The Wimbledon Society Museum of Local History, the latter containing a wonderfully comprehensive display, detailing Wimbledon's rich history over the years. The Club and Lecture Hall opened in 1859, and has housed the museum, privately funded and run by volunteers, since 1916. Opening hours are Saturday and Sunday 2.30-5.00 pm.

Use the zebra crossing to gain the left-hand pavement and when you get to the High Street turn left. Cross at the lights and stroll past the shops to a roundabout at Church Road, where you turn right.

On the opposite corner is the Dog and Fox, one of the village's popular watering-holes, and the starting point for regular columns of horse riders setting forth from the adjacent stables for a hack on the common. In the days before car travel horses for the London coach, via Clapham, were stabled here. Although the present building is Victorian, there has been an inn on this site since at least 1617, when the name was recorded as My Lord's Arms. Facing the pub, and adorned with a central bell tower, is the Old Fire Station, which was in use from 1890 to 1907. On the corner of Church Road are two tile-hung 17th-century buildings, both well-established restaurants. In keeping with today's fashions the right-hand one once served as a coffee-house, opened in 1877, known as The Welcome.

Carry on along Church Road, passing an interesting variety of shops, a tiny courtyard containing the charming 18th-century Walnut Tree Cottages, and Belvedere Square. Press on ahead to a mini-roundabout, where you turn right.

The Old Fire Station

Down the hill, but not on your route, are the world-famous courts of the All England Lawn Tennis Club, and the Wimbledon Lawn Tennis Museum, shop, and café. Opening hours are 10-5 daily. Nearer at hand, but tucked well away from the road, is the Old Rectory, Wimbledon's oldest building, which dates from about 1500. In the 16th century Lord Burghley occupied this fine house with its Tudor turrets, walls two to three feet thick, and panelled dining hall, and his name lives on in nearby Burghley Road. The best view that you can get of the Rectory is from St Mary's churchyard, the next stop on your walk.

Before reaching the next mini-roundabout cross with care and continue on the left-hand pavement to Stag Lodge and St Mary's church.

The stag that gazes inquisitively from the parapet of Stag Lodge is a 1980s replacement for the original, which was accidentally broken during removal

Stag Lodge and St Mary's church spire

for safekeeping in World War II. This lodge served as the gatehouse to the last of Wimbledon's four manor houses, which stood on or around this hill-top site from 1588, when the Elizabethan manor house of Sir Thomas Cecil first appeared, to 1949 when Earl Spencer's once-fine house, sadly dilapidated, faced demolition.

St Mary's church occupies an ancient religious site where a church may well have stood in Anglo-Saxon times. This was replaced in the late 13th century with a small medieval church topped with a spire, and again by a much grander Georgian building in 1788. The present handsome structure of 1843, a landmark often featured by the TV cameras during the tennis tournament, is the work of Sir George Gilbert Scott.

Pass Stag Lodge and the ultra-modern church hall, then press on ahead along Arthur Road, passing a most unusual domed house, formerly the Artesian Well. This is a rare survivor of the outbuildings of Earl Spencer's manor house, and provided water from a borehole over 500ft deep.

Take the next left to follow Home Park Road, with Wimbledon Park spread out to your left and a succession of splendid houses opposite, well placed to admire the scenery.

Although the park is now hemmed in by houses and blocks of flats, some idea of the magnificent view enjoyed from the manor house can be appreciated from here. Earl Spencer's huge Wimbledon Park estate stretched to

West Hill and Tibbet's Corner, and then bordered Wimbledon Common along what is now Parkside.

After just over ½ mile turn into the park through an obvious sign-posted gate and descend steps (or use the adjacent sloping path) towards a playground. Keep to the tarmac path as it weaves through this children's delight, then leave through a gate (toilets on the right) and carry on beside the lake.

Renowned landscape garden designer Lancelot 'Capability' Brown laid out Wimbledon Park for the lord of the manor in the 1760s, transforming what had been formal gardens into a more natural scene, with areas of woodland, a long winding entrance drive from the Portsmouth Road, and two streams that flowed down from the higher ground of Wimbledon Common dammed to form a thirty-acre lake.

After passing a boat storage enclosure turn right then immediately left along a tarmac path with a Capital Ring sign pointing the way. Follow this path alongside a tree-lined fence, with a great swathe of open grass to your right, until you reach a corner. From here you can either strike out slightly left across the grass, or take the perimeter path, to leave the park through a gate and turn right along Wimbledon Park Road. Continue past the Wimbledon Park estate flats and then Southfields library, which has public toilets, except when closed on Thursday and Sunday.

Carry on the short distance to Southfields station and the end of your walk, or for refreshment turn right into Replingham Road for one or two pubs and cafés.

The Lake, Wimbledon Park

Eagle House, Wimbledon Village (Walk 28)

SW19

28 Wimbledon Common

Limitless acres to run about in, lots of hide-and-seek trees, scenery, woods, and wildlife, and the welcome sight of the Windmill café

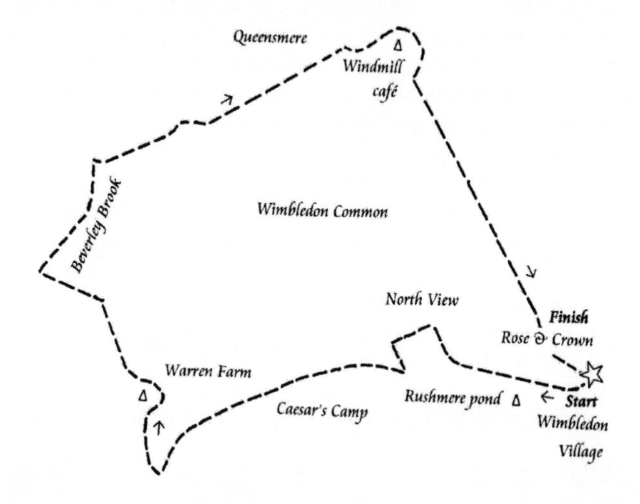

Distance	4½ miles.
Time	2½ hours.
Terrain	Gravel paths and some rough tracks, which may be muddy in wet weather.
Food and drink	Pubs and cafés in Wimbledon Village, Windmill café, Fox and Grapes pub.
Toilets	Next to Windmill café.
Start and Finish	Rose and Crown Hotel, High Street Wimbledon Village. Bus 93. Buses 200 and 493 both stop nearby in Wimbledon Village.

With your back to the Rose and Crown cross the road and go straight ahead, passing several shops including Wimbledon Books and Music. This is still the High Street. Take the first right at The Green, then after 25 yards cross the road and take the wide shared path and cycle track diagonally right across the common, with Rushmere Pond on your left. Cross Cannizaro Road and continue on this broad gravel track to a junction of roads at West Side Common. Here you will find the Fox and Grapes pub. Turn right to follow West Place, alongside a row of picturesque cottages. The road turns sharply to the left; follow it round, now on North View.

Glance up to see the sunrise and sunset in relief on next-door gable ends, while just round the corner are two blue plaques fixed to neighbouring house fronts. At number 9, 'Ernst Chain, Developer of Penicillin' and at number 8 'Josephine Butler, Champion of Women's Rights'. For many years this house sported a huge stuffed bear as a welcome by the front door.

Shortly you turn sharp left again, now on Camp View, past a group of substantial houses blessed with outsize windows for the occupants to enjoy the rural scene hereabouts. Turn right to pass the Wimbledon Common golf club, and then keep left along Camp Road. Follow this quiet backwater for ¼ mile until it comes to an end at a gate. Maintain your direction along a footpath located to the right of this gate.

Look out for a plaque to the right of the path denoting the eastern boundary of an earthwork known as 'Caesar's Camp', which is actually an Iron Age hill fort about 800 feet in diameter and covering around 12 acres. Your path goes right through the middle of it. The earthworks used to be much more prominent until John Sawbridge-Erle-Drax, a member of the Dorset landowning family who had inherited this estate, made plans in the 1870s to build houses here, and had felled trees and levelled the ramparts and ditches of the camp before being stopped by the Commons Conservators. Now you

Footpath through Caesar's Camp

have the greens and fairways of the golf course for company on both sides, and on a clear day views to the far-off Surrey hills.

Follow this delightful fenced way for ½ mile to arrive at a crossing track. Turn right here, with Beverley Meads nature reserve on your left. The path soon crosses a ditch and climbs gently through woodland to arrive near the buildings of Warren Farm. At the end of a garden fence turn left and then cross the farm entrance way to join another gravel track, where after a few yards you must bear left on a vehicle-width descending track. After barely ¼ mile you will come to a major crossing by-way. This is Robin Hood Ride (or Road) and one of the common's few cycling routes, onto which you turn left and continue arrow-straight towards a white gate and bridge. Turn right just before the bridge, from where your route is enlivened by the company of the fast-flowing Beverley Brook.

Rising in the suburban slopes of Stoneleigh and Sutton, the brook flows alongside Wimbledon Common and then through Richmond Park to join the Thames at Barn Elms, near Putney. The 6½ mile long Beverley Brook Walk, starting at New Malden station and following the brook through some of south-west London's most attractive green spaces, offers a chance to spot some interesting wildlife, including an occasional kingfisher in Richmond Park.

Continue alongside the brook, passing a Putney parish boundary stone dated 1861. After ¼ mile, when a sports field comes into view, turn sharp right then after 20 yards bear left (your walk now coincides with the Capital Ring, a 78 mile route linking many of London's green spaces, as far as Wimbledon Windmill). Within a few yards go left on another wide track, eventually passing a war memorial away to your left. After nearly ¼ mile, at a junction, turn right, uphill. Fork left at the next junction, tackle an uphill stretch (not too arduous), then cross two golf fairways, keeping a good watch for whizzing golf balls. Immediately after the second fairway keep left on the main downhill track, again with a Capital Ring arrow, which descends to the banks of Queensmere, one of nine ponds on the commons. Now turn right on a gently sloping uphill track, at the top of which you turn left for the Windmill Museum, café, and toilets.

Queensmere

In olden times Wimbledon Common was a place where 'commoners' would graze their animals and gather wood and furze. This rustic peace was much disturbed when in 1860 the National Rifle Association held their first meeting here, with Queen Victoria firing the first shot (a bull's eye). The great success of this event finally required a move, thirty year later, to Bisley. Nowadays the common is better known for recreation and as a wildlife habitat, With 900 acres designated as a Site of Special Scientific Interest (SSSI) and Special Area of Conservation (SAC).

After a break here turn right to pass the Windmill Museum, where you can see the workings of this restored hollow-post mill of 1817 (open April-October Saturdays 2-5, Sundays and public holidays 11-5), then turn right again.

The Information centre, which you will find to your right here, contains an absorbing display of the common's wildlife, natural features, and history,

The Windmill on Wimbledon Common

including the lord of the manor's plans for enclosure in the 1860s, leading to a long legal battle, finally resolved by an Act of Parliament of 1871 transferring responsibility to a Board of Conservators.

Ahead of you now is a barrier; go round it and continue on a wide, well-used way. Take the first track off to the left, marked by two white posts, which leads along the edge of woodland, with open grassland on your left. Press on along this track, ignoring all side turnings. Soon you will pass Bluegate gravel pit, a shallow pond which may be bone-dry in summer, half-hidden amongst the low woodland to your left. Passing an old fenced cattle pound in a leafy bower beside the path, you now cross Cannizaro Road and continue through an avenue of lime trees to reach the Wimbledon war memorial. Bear left to the High Street and the welcome sight of the Rose and Crown, your final destination.

SW19

29 Cannizaro Park

Superb trees, gardens, and seasonal blooms, a maze of paths and wealth of hiding places for young ones, fresh air and beautiful surroundings

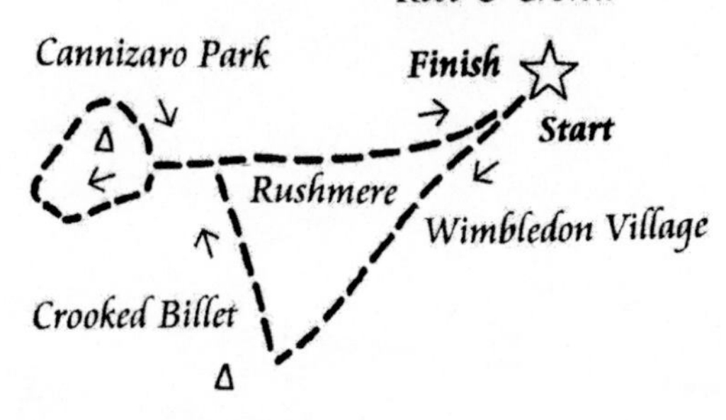

Distance	2 miles.
Time	1½ hours.
Terrain	Paved or gravel paths, with a few steps in Cannizaro Park, easily avoided.
Food and drink	Pubs and cafes in Wimbledon Village, 3 pubs on Wimbledon Common.
Toilets	Cannizaro Park.
Start and Finish	Rose and Crown Hotel, High Street Wimbledon Village. Bus 93, also 200 and 493 stop nearby.

With your back to the Rose and Crown cross the High Street and go straight ahead, passing Wimbledon Books and Music.

On your left are two stone lions, reproductions of those which previously graced the front door of Wimbledon Lodge, Southside, home of General Sir Henry Murray. At the start of Murray Road (which you will cross in a moment) is a crescent, which formed the entrance drive to his mansion. After the lions, the next building is Claremont House, built in 1650. The side wing at one time contained a general store, and more recently, a popular café.

Follow the pavement along Southside Common, with an avenue of chestnut trees and a broad expanse of the common to your right.

On the way, look out for several notable houses which include Lauriston Cottage, dating from 1675, thankfully spared when Lauriston House, once the home of anti-slavery campaigner William Wilberforce, was swept away; South Lodge, built in 1840; and Rushmere, which started life as a farm house in 1788.

Rose and Crown, Wimbledon Village

Carry on, crossing several roads, until you arrive at the impressive buildings of King's College School.

King's College School moved here in 1897 from the Strand. Famous former pupils include Dante Gabriel Rossetti, the Pre-Raphaelite artist, and Charles Dickens's son, Charles Dickens Jr. Just beyond the school stands Southside House, where a guided tour of the richly-furnished interior will reveal such secrets as the room where Emma Hamilton is said to have entertained Admiral Nelson with her artistic but naughty 'attitudes'. A treasure trove of works of art and personal mementoes, the house, which was built in the late 1600s, is still looked after by descendants of the Pennington-Mellor-Munthe family.

Cross the road at the pedestrian crossing and go half-right to follow Westside Common. A few yards away to your left, and well worth a short detour, are two ever-popular pubs, the Hand in Hand and Crooked Billet, and a very attractive cluster of cottages.

As you continue along Westside Common, you will pass Chester House, dating from about 1670, and in the 1700s the home of John Horne Tooke, politician and wit. Once across Chester Road you come to some houses from the 18th century; Westside House, and then tucked away down a lane, the Dutch-style cottages of Hanford Row.

Eventually you will arrive at the gates of Cannizaro Park, just beyond Cannizaro House Hotel. Go through the gates into the park, and pass the 'teapot' fountain. Soon you turn left, with a small aviary to your right, to find yourself in front of the hotel's terrace (a grand place for a special occasion afternoon tea) where you turn right.

Cannizaro Park gained its unusual name when Count St Antonio, occupant of what was then Warren House, succeeded to the title of Duke of Cannizzaro, Sicily, in 1832. Although he returned to Italy, the name is still with us today, albeit with just one 'z'. Successive owners have added to the fine collection of exotic trees and shrubs to create the beautiful surroundings that we enjoy today. The estate was finally purchased by Wimbledon Corporation and opened to the public in 1949, and is still maintained to a high standard, with breathtaking displays of spring flowers, azaleas, camellias, and rhododendrons in the woodland away to the left, and vivid colours of red, gold, and yellow on the autumn trees.

Cannizaro Park

Take the wide path, flanked by sweeping, spacious lawns, down to a duck-pond. Carry on past the pond, go ahead up a short gravelly slope, then turn right to stroll along an avenue of mature trees. At a junction turn right (the rose garden straight ahead is a delight) and continue to another junction (toilets to the left here) where you go right, to find yourself back at the aviary. Turn left past the ever-pouring fountain and leave the park. With your back to the gates cross the road and strike out half-right across the common towards Wimbledon Village, passing Rushmere Pond on the way. Soon you come to The Green, a triangle of attractive old houses, to the right of which is the High Street and the completion of your walk.

As you return to the village's bustle and activity, take a moment to admire Eagle House, next-door neighbour to the Rose and Crown. This handsome Jacobean manor house dates from 1613, having been built by Robert Bell, a founder of the East India Company. In recent years it has been carefully restored, and ranks as Wimbledon's second-oldest house.

Rushmere Pond, Wimbledon Common

SW15, SW19

30 Putney Heath

A pleasant heathland stroll, and a chance to ride your bike on recognised cycle tracks, followed by tea, a drink or meal at the Windmill Café, Green Man, or Telegraph

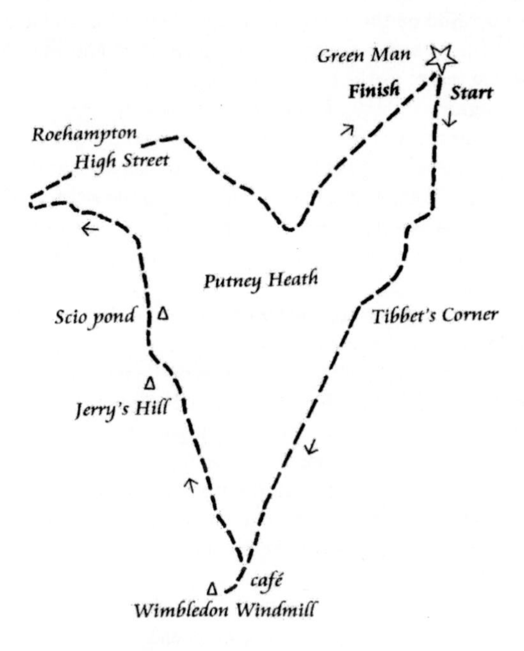

Distance	4¼ miles.
Time	2 hours.
Terrain	Pavements and gravel paths; no steep gradients.
Food and drink	Green Man pub, a tea stall nearby, café at Wimbledon Windmill, The Telegraph pub.
Toilets	Windmill café, Putney Heath bus terminus.
Start and Finish	Green Man, Putney Heath (top of Putney Hill) Buses 14, 37, 39, 85, 93, 170, 424, 493.

From the Green Man pub, walk to the junction with Putney Hill, which you cross and then turn right, uphill. Cross Putney Heath Lane and then keep left, still on Putney Hill, with several large blocks of flats on your left, and woods to the right. A few yards after a post box by Ross Court look out for an ancient boundary stone inscribed 'Wandsworth Parish 1787 Thos Woodward Thos Rooke Churchwardens'. Shortly after this you arrive at West Hill. Turn right and follow the pavement as it curves to the right, then turn left under the roadway at Tibbet's Corner roundabout.

In the 1700s this locality was a favourite haunt of robbers and highwaymen, notably the notorious Jerry Abershawe, whose reign of terror lasted until he was finally caught and hanged on Kennington Common and his body afterwards displayed on the gallows on Putney Heath. Tibbet incidentally was not of this ilk; he was gatekeeper on Earl Spencer's Wimbledon Park estate, and lived in the lodge nearby.

Turn left again, and then follow the pavement straight ahead to ascend a wide tarmac slope, with the heath surrounding you. A gravel track known as Ladies' Mile threads forward ahead of you. Keeping company with this track for ¾ mile, passing King's Mere pond away to the right, will finally bring you to Wimbledon Windmill. Here you will find a café, toilets, Information centre, and Windmill Museum (open April-October Saturdays 2-5, Sundays and public holidays 11-5).

Built in 1817 as a hollow-post mill, with the driven shaft from the sails contained within the hollowed-out supporting pole, the windmill originally ground flour until in 1864 when the lord of the manor of Wimbledon, Earl Spencer, tried to enclose the common it was converted to six cottages. Now restored and open as a museum, the windmill and adjacent café are the focal point of Wimbledon Common and a reassuring sight if you are not quite sure of your bearings on the 1100 acres of heath and common.

From the windmill cross the car park entrance road to a Capital Ring sign, and follow the green pointing finger past another old boundary stone. Although it has no inscription, it is one of several marking the old boundary of Putney parish. Go slightly left across the grass to join a track, close to the one on which you arrived here, and then keep left on a wide track which you follow for ½ mile, keeping to the left at a Y-junction. On the way you will pass Jerry's Hill, the spot where Jerry Abershawe's corpse was said to have been hung as a warning to other footpads and highwaymen.

Eventually the path dives down through a subway under the A3 Kingston Road. Bear left at a junction and continue on this path as it converges on the road and then sweeps right, back into trees, to arrive at Scio Pond. After passing the pond, fork left at a junction and follow this shared path and cycle track until just before meeting Ponsonby Road you must bear left on a narrow path that heads for Holy Trinity church.

George Fellowes-Prynne was the architect of this fine church of 1896-98. The Bath stone spire rises to over 200 feet, and the interior contains much of beauty, including an imposing stone screen separating nave and chancel. The church is Grade II* listed.

Scio Pond, Putney Heath

Do not pass the church; instead turn right along Ponsonby Road then left at Medfield Street, passing Elizabeth Place, a terrace of verdantly-swathed cottages. Before reaching the drinking fountain cross the road and at the bus stop follow a passageway, Blackford's Path, to ascend a short flight of steps to Roehampton High Street (to avoid the steps simply carry on past the bus stop to swing right into the High Street).

Many fine mansions adorned the countryside around Roehampton Village in the 17th and 18th centuries, including Roehampton House, built by Thomas Archer in 1710-12. In later years many of these grand houses were converted for use as institutions of one sort or another, such as Roehampton University and Queen Mary's Hospital, which incorporated Archer's building. Rural seclusion disappeared forever when the London County Council embarked on the 'cottages' of the huge Dover House estate between the wars, and then in the 1950s the Alton estate's slab blocks of housing appeared.

With The Angel pub opposite turn right to follow the High Street. Note the charming Tweedside Cottages on your left. Go past the line of shops and keep on ahead to make acquaintance once again with Putney

Heath. Cross to the left-hand pavement and continue past Dover House Road. After passing a zebra crossing and bus stop turn right to follow Telegraph Road. Pass Crossroads Cottage, tucked away in a woodland clearing, and then a cricket pitch. Carry on ahead, crossing Heathview Gardens and Portsmouth Road to arrive facing The Telegraph pub.

In 1796 the Admiralty set up a shutter-operated telegraph signal station here, in a line of communication that stretched to Portsmouth and Plymouth, to warn of any possible French attack. A message from London could reach Portsmouth in 15 minutes on a clear day.

Another interesting structure that has now vanished was the Fireproof House, invented by David Hartley in 1772-73, and demonstrated to King George III and Queen Charlotte, who apparently were served breakfast in perfect safety while a fire burned in the room below. A monument to this innovation, complete with a fulsome inscription, still stands in the trees near the main road. The mansion that sprang up in its place, Wildcroft (owned by publisher Sir George Newnes) has itself been replaced by the flats of Wildcroft Manor, which still retain the mansion's ornate iron gateway.

Turn left to follow Wildcroft Road, noting the old cattle pound, a place where stray animals would be 'impounded', in the trees to your right as you approach the 17th-century Green Man and the end of this tour of Putney Heath.

Cattle pound at the Green Man